LIFE IN EGYPT
IN ANCIENT TIMES

LIFE IN EGYPT
IN ANCIENT TIMES

Bernard Romant
Translated by J. Smith

Minerva

Contents

Crédits : Alinari/Viollet : 8 - 117. — D.R. : 15 - 28 - 41. —
Dulevant : 98 - 119. — Fiore : 59. — Giraudon : 4 - 6 -
7 - 10 - 16 - 18 - 19 - 24 - 31 - 33 - 48 - 49 - 50 - 52 -
56 - 74a - 76 - 94 - 95 - 99 - 103 - 106 - 114 - 118 -
120 - 122 - 133 - 141 - 142 - 143. — Harlingue : 136. —
Metropolitan Museum, New York : 42 - 43 - 75 - 111.
— S.E.F. : 66 - 78 - 102 - 107. — Unedi : End papers -
20 - 25 - 26 - 34 - 51 - 54 - 60 - 68 - 70 - 71 - 72 - 74b -
81 - 85 - 88 - 92 - 97 - 100 - 101 - 104 - 105 - 108 - 109 -
116 - 124 - 126 - 129. — Viollet : 2 - 11 - 12 - 13 - 17
- 22 - 23 - 35 - 37 - 45 - 47c - 58 - 59 - 63 - 73 - 90 -
110 - 130 - 132 - 139.

Right, this stele-cum-votive table (XII Dynasty) reveals some symbolic types of ancient Egypt.

© *Editions Minerva, S.A. Genève, 1978/81*
Achevé d'imprimer le 10 mai 1986
par Milanostampa s.p.a., Farigliano (Cuneo)
Printed in Italy

THE LAND OF THE PHARAOHS

If there is one place where the soul is seized with a kind of "sacred terror", it is surely Egypt, the land of the Pharaohs, which has lain sleeping for thousands of years under the slowly shifting sands.

Now that temples and tombs have been uncovered by Western archaeologists, the eternal sun-god, Râ, once more sheds his radiance out over this hieratic and motionless world. All along the banks of the sluggish Nile so beloved of Herodotus, the figures of Ramses, Thoutmosis, Akenaton and the pure profile of Nefertiti have all now re-appeared before the eyes of men.

Yet the Egypt that gave birth to the civilization which radiated throughout the world of Antiquity may have still other tombs hidden in some sacred place—tombs in which gilded mummies still sleep, watched over by the strange eye of the black, jackal-headed Anubis, god of the dead.

In this book we shall not disturb the sleep of the granite gods and Pharaohs behind the columns, shaped like papyrus and lotus, of their temples. Our purpose is more modest: it is to bring to life, from the depths of the sands, the men and women of Egypt. Nobles, priests, merchants, fellahs: it is *their* lives that we wish to show to the Western reader, with all their cares, sufferings, joys, with their moments of greatness and also their more humdrum day-to-day concerns.

In these few pages we shall not try to summarize the vast body of documentation which exists on ancient Egypt. But we should recall that the Empire of the Pharaohs lasted nearly 3,000 years. Historians generally agree that 31 dynasties succeeded each other on the throne, though this figure has been arrived at somewhat arbitrarily. Rather than going into detail we shall concentrate on a limited number of periods, each of which gave Egypt something new.

For example, the first and second dynasties form the Thinite period, which began about 3,100 BC, with the union of the kingdoms of Upper and Lower Egypt under the authority of the first Pharaoh Menes. Menes was the first king whose sole and exclusive title was "Pharaoh". This term means "palace", as it was felt that the king was too great to be named. He wore the *Pschent,* or double crown, thus merging the white crown, with its cobra emblem, and the red crown of Lower Egypt. Menes lived in Memphis, as did his immediate successors.

The Old Empire covers the third, fourth, fifth and sixth dynasties. This is the period, from 2,770-2,200 BC, which included the reigns of so many remarkable sovereigns: Djeser, Cheops, Chephren and Mykerinos. It was during this period, moreover, that the first great Egyptian monuments were erected, from the tiered pyramid of Sakkarah to the three great pyramids of Gizeh.

Then came an intermediate period, with five dynasties. The Middle Empire lasted until the 13th dynasty. The capital city was moved to Thebes and the heightened authority of the Pharaoh was accompanied by immense prosperity and a flowering of the arts and sciences.

A second intermediate period, from the 13th to the 17th dynasties, was rather decadent.

The New Empire, which lasted from 1567-1085 BC, comprised the 18th to the 20th dynasties. This was the age of Ahmes I, Hatschepsout the female Pharaoh, Akhenaton the Pharaoh with the goat-like features who sought to replace the traditional forms of worship, the Ramessides, from Ramses III to XI. Egypt was now at the peak of its territorial power. The Valley of the Kings, the Valley of the Queens and the Valley of the Nobles, opposite Luxor, were hollowed out of the hard earth; fabulous tombs were built and were filled with immense riches, while prestigious temples were built at Deir-el Bahari, Karnak and Luxor. Enormous technological difficulties were overcome in the construction of the obelisks which towered above these edifices.

During the Lower Period, 1085-341 BC, a divided Egypt was already well on the way towards decline, and would soon fall a prey to invaders. There were Sudanese, Libyan, Deltaic and Persian Pharaohs, interspersed with the last native Pharaohs.

Then Alexander the Great also conquered the Nile Valley. After his death one of his generals, Ptolemy, founded a new dynasty, that of the Hellenistic period.

Egypt later passed through a Roman period, from 30 BC to 395 AD, a Byzantine period lasting until 642 and a Moslem period which ended in modern times, in 1805.

Here we are concerned only with ancient Egypt, the Egypt in which the people living along the banks of Nile knew only one master, the divine Pharaoh—the ruler who was held in such respect that he could be called by no other name.

1. MARRIAGE, FAMILY AND CHILDREN

MARRIAGE

If the authority of Diodorus can be credited, women were indulged with greater privileges in Egypt than in any other country. He even affirms that part of the agreement entered into at the time of marriage was that the wife should have control over her husband, and that no objection should be made to her *commands*. However, it does not seem that such authority went beyond household management and its daily problems.

The tomb-paintings contain few pictures of marriage ceremonies. But we do have several marriage settlements of the Ptolemaic period in the demotic character. The conditions were that if the husband took a second wife, he should pay a fine to the first, whose eldest son was to be heir to the property. In the "bubble" of a fresco a father recommends to his son a course of action which says a great deal about the atmosphere in the average Egyptian home! He says: "Above all, never watch over your wife while she is working in the house".

Women of high rank enjoyed every right pertaining to property, and had legal status which enabled them to buy, sell and take legal action. They often played a part in affairs of State, performing a kind of political role. The Queens of Egypt sometimes wielded exceptional influence as advisers to the Pharaohs. This is readily understandable if one considers that legitimacy of descent was established through women. Two such queens governed Egypt alone for several months at a time. Hatshepsout, in particular, is a striking example of a woman-Pharaoh: this powerful, dynamic woman wore the double crown and—perhaps to further emphasize her authority—was even known, from time to time, to wear that highly masculine emblem of the Pharaohs, the traditional false beard.

Diodorus informs us the Egyptians were not restricted to any number of wives, but that every one married as many as he chose, with the exception of the priesthood, who were by law confined to one consort. It does not, however, appear that

Two illustrious couples: right, an official from Memphis and his young wife; the woman in the couple on the left is none other than Nefertiti.

7

they generally took advantage of this privilege; and Herodotus affirms that throughout Egypt it was customary to marry only one wife. There may well have been economic and budgetary reasons for such a limitation. After all, wives are expensive, in any country in the world!

As for marriage between the Pharaohs and persons related to them by blood, they were not rare, as may be deduced from Diodorus, and from the paintings and sculptures of Upper and Lower Egypt. This exceedingly ancient custom guaranteed the authenticity of descent, which is never so completely proved as by the female line. It moreover provides a fine illustration of the practical wisdom of the Egyptians. If necessary, of course, the example of Osiris marrying his sister Isis would suffice as historical evidence of the custom.

THE ROMANTIC SIDE OF LOVE

Besides considerations of family and property, which figured prominently in most marriages in ancient Egypt, there was a notable element of romantic love, as can be seen from a number of love-poems which have come down to us. It is also made evident by the obviously affectionate poses in which married couples and their children are portrayed in ancient Egyptian art; indeed, one is inclined to say that such external signs of warmth and love, particularly among married couples, are perhaps unique in the art of the ancient world. Some authors suggest that there may have been as many marriages based on true love as there were marriages resulting from more business-like, pecuniary arrangements between the parents concerned, or from negotiations between them.

Love poetry was a major literary genre in ancient Egypt. It has left us some remarkable outpourings of sentiment, on the part of both young lovers and married people. For example, a young man was full of anguish because he had not seen his "sister" (this term was commonly used to denote "mistress" or "loved one") for a whole week:

For a week past I have not seen my sister,
and a sickness has invaded me;
and my body has become heavy,
I am oblivious to my own self.
If the chief physicians come to me,
my heart is not content with their remedies.
What will revive me is to hear the words "Here she is!"
Her name is what will lift me up.
My health is to see her come back to me;
when I see her then I am better again...
When I embrace her she drives away all evil—
But she has been away from me for seven whole days!

Similarly, an oft-quoted passage from a poem written by a widower to his dead wife, about the year 1,000 BC, illustrates the kind of passions felt by spouses for each other. After his wife's death the widower fell gravely ill; a soothsayer told him that his illness was due to his mistreatment of his wife during her lifetime, and that he had to write to her in order to placate her wounded spirit. The following passage is from the deeply moving letter he wrote in response to this request:

"What evil have I done to you, that I should find myself in this wretched state? What then have I done to you, that you should lay your hand upon me, when no evil was done to you? You became my wife when I was young, and I was with you. I was appointed to all manner of offices, and I was with you. I did not forsake you or cause your heart any sorrow... Behold, when I commanded the foot-soldiers of Pharaoh, together with his chariot force, I did cause you to come that they might fall down before you, and they brought all manner of good things to present to you. When you were ill with the sickness which afflicted you, I went to the Chief Physician and he made you your medicine, he did everything that you said he should do. When I had to accompany Pharaoh on his journey to the south, my thoughts were with you, and I spent those eight months without caring to eat or drink. When I returned to Memphis, I besought the Pharaoh and betook myself to you, and I greatly mourned

for you with the people of my house."

What a splendid example of conjugal love! Yet this particular wife, though idolized and cherished by her husband, was still not satisfied, and continued to torment him from the Great Beyond!

SEXUAL MORALS

Even if the great love two spouses felt for each other was not always so evident, so keen and so

Below: this ivory statuette depicts a concubine.

constant as in the case just described, even if concubines interfered in household affairs— apparently a fairly common occurrence—there were very few harems, if only because of the high cost of supporting their inmates. And virtue was certainly encouraged, *inter alia,* by the pervasive and powerful moral influence of the priesthood.

The Books of Wisdom, containing the reputed maxims of sages such as Imhotep, Ani and Ptahhotep, give numerous warnings against the perils of seductive women. The following is a frequently quoted passage:

"Beware of a woman from strange parts, whose city is not known. When she comes do not look at her or know her. She is as the eddy in deep water, the depth of which is unknown. The woman whose husband is far off writes to thee every day. If no witness is near her she stands up and spreads out her net with which to ensnare thee. O fearful crime to listen to her!"

Morality among the Egyptian proletariat seems to have been very low; indeed, assaulting "strange women" appears to have been a common offence at that level of society.

Even when one makes due allowance for the sense of caricature for which the ancient Egyptians are so remarkable, one cannot fail to be shocked to learn that a tomb of the twentieth dynasty contained a book of obscene pictures, annotated by a caricaturist; one is inclined, in fact, to wonder about the morality of a nation which could supply the dead with this kind of reading material for the long journey into the unkown. Moreover, an ancient sacred book which gives an account of the heavenly joys reserved for the Pharaoh on departing this life says that he will be free to "take wives away from their husbands" as often as he likes!

But one should not complain: after all, if such lascivious joys cannot be sampled until one reaches the world to come, then the morals of society are well protected!

Right and above, another three couples, young, confident and harmonious.

TREATMENT OF WOMEN

Egyptian women were not kept in the same secluded manner as those of ancient Greece. They were treated very differently, and in a manner much more worthy of a civilised people.

The sculptures of both temples and tombs illustrate extensively the important role of women in everyday life. At some of the public festivals women were expected to attend,—not alone, like the Moslem women at a mosque, but in company with their husbands or relations; and the wives of priests, as well as the queen, joined in performing the ceremonies of the temple: women were eligible for the offices of serving the gods.

Wives were always treated with courtesy. If it did happen that, in certain banquets, they stayed on one side of the room, with the men on the other, it was not through any feeling of disdain towards them; in fact they were waited upon and generally treated in exactly the same way as all the other guests.

That they were not restricted in the use of wine, and in the enjoyment of other luxuries, is evident

from the frescoes which represent their feasts; and the painters, in illustrating this fact, have sometimes sacrificed their gallantry to a love of caricature. Some call the servants to support them as they sit, others with difficulty prevent themselves from falling on those behind them: a basin is brought too late by a reluctant servant, and the faded flower, which is ready to drop from their heated hands, is intended to be characteristic of their own sensations.

Such a scene indicates clearly that the weak sex was not required to show more restraint, or even more virtue, than the strong sex.

Women endured the same penalties and punishments as men under Egyptian law. For example, they could be beaten with sticks. When a woman committed a crime, she risked capital punishment. However, they took care to determine whether or not she was pregnant; if she was, the carrying out of the sentence was delayed until after the birth of the child.

But some of their laws regarding the female sex were cruel and unjustifiable. A woman who had committed adultery was sentenced to lose her nose, upon the principle that being the most conspicuous feature, and the chief, or at least an indispensable, ornament of the face, its loss would be most severely felt, and be the greatest detriment to her personal charms; and the man was condemned to receive a beating of one thousand blows. But if it was proved that he had used force against a free woman, he was doomed to a cruel and inhuman punishment.

CHILDREN

Love for their children was one of the characteristic traits of the ancient Egyptians, and they never missed a single opportunity to indulge this feeling; sometimes they did so even ostentatiously. Displays of parental affection were never thought to be out of place. Indeed, the most prominent priest would not feign indifference towards his offspring, even if his priestly duties were to suffer as a result. It is only logical, therefore, that

13

great importance was attached to education.

In the education of youth they were particularly strict; and "they knew," says Plato, "that children ought to be early accustomed to such gestures, looks, and motions as are decent and proper; and not to be suffered either to hear or learn any verses and songs than those which are calculated to inspire them with virtue; and they consequently took care that every dance and ode introduced at their feasts or sacrifices should be subject to certain regulations." They particularly inculcated respect for old age; and the fact of this being required towards strangers necessarily argues a great regard for the person of a parent; for we are informed that, like the Lacedæmonians, they required every young man to give place to his superiors in years, and even if seated, to rise on their approach: a son, for example, was not expected to sit in the presence of his father without express permission.

The duties of the Egyptian princes were also austere. One of these was "fanbearer on the right of the king". As fanbearers, they accompanied him while he was seated on his throne, or in processions to the temple; and in this capacity they followed his chariot on foot as he celebrated his triumphant return from battle. Nor did they lay aside their insignia of office in time of war; and sometimes in the heat of battle, whether mounted in cars or engaged on foot, they carried them in their hand or slung behind them.

They also had to carry the monarch about in his palanquin or royal chair, and, as a distinguishing mark of princely rank, they wore a badge hanging from the side of the head, perhaps intended to cover and enclose the lock of hair which, among the Egyptians, was the sign of extreme youth, and the usual emblem of the god Harpocrates.

However, the Egyptians always expected a great deal from their children, and, on the whole, their expectations were fulfilled. This was true both in the upper classes and among the popular masses, as can be seen from many of the sculptures at Thebes.

The same custom prevailed among the Egyptians regarding children as with the Moslems and other Eastern people; no distinction being made between their offspring by a wife or any other woman, and all equally enjoying the rights of inheritance: for since they considered a child indebted to the

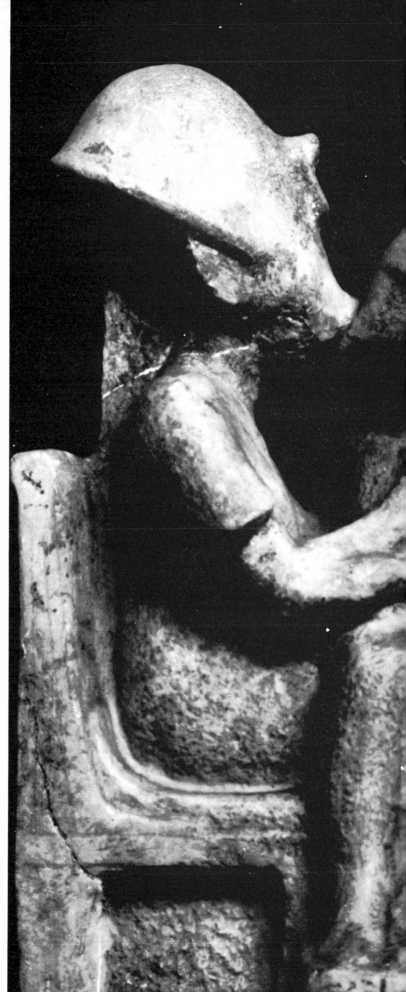

father for its existence, and the mother to be "little more than a nurse," it seemed unjust to deny equal rights to all their progeny.

Yet the Egyptians, as we have seen, were wise enough to consider that the female line of descent alone was reliable, as it alone could be definitely proved.

The clothes of children of the lower classes were very simple; and, as Diodorus informs us, the expenses incurred in feeding and clothing them amounted to a mere trifle. "They feed them", he says, "very lightly, and at an incredibly small cost; giving them a little meal of the coarsest and cheapest kind, the pith of the papyrus, baked under the ashes, with the roots and stalks of some marsh weeds, either raw, boiled, or roasted; and since most of them are brought up, on account of the mildness of the climate, without shoes, and indeed without any other clothing, the whole expense incurred by the parents does not exceed 20 drachmæ each; and this frugality is the true reason of the populousness of Egypt." But the children of the higher orders were often dressed like grown persons, with a loose robe reaching to the ankles, and sandals.

When the child had become a little older it used to be put astride its mother's shoulder—an apparently uncomfortable position, in which it had to cling to its mother's hair in order to keep its balance.

As one might expect, education was taken further

Left, a highly symbolic bas-relief: it shows a god (a ram) modelling the figure of a child on a potter's wheel! Facing and above, two moving pictures of motherhood and a family, apparently a very united one. These two items are extremely ancient.

in some households than in others. Diodorus, for example, tells us that "the children of the priests knew two kinds of script, that which went by the name of "sacred" and a more common variety."

Much emphasis was laid on the study of geometry and arithmetic. In the words of the same historian, "the annual flood of the Nile causes such drastic changes in the appearance of the landscape, thus giving rise to endless and varied arguments among neighbours about the precise extent of their land, that it would be difficult for anyone to resolve these problems without having recourse to the methods of geometry". A fine example of judicious pragmatism!

Among the masses of the people, however, education was dispensed only to the extent thought necessary for the performance of each person's occupation. Literature was addressed only to a small élite, and, according to Diodorus, "to the best of the craftsmen".

The Egyptians therefore followed no strict rule in their educational curricula. The parents were the ones who decided on the level of education to be given to their children, in the light of their future occupation and their aptitude for work.

GAMES AND TOYS

Egyptian parents, being aware, as we have seen, of the importance of education, did not confine their attention solely to their children's formal studies. They realized the importance of games for the formation of both body and character. The recreation of children was thus designed to enhance the physical condition by means of exercises and to stimulate the mind through laughter, jest and imitation. As soon as their age allowed, children were encouraged to take part in competitions or games: jumping, running, throwing the weight or the ball, and also wrestling. Merit was encouraged and rewarded.

The ancient Egyptians had a number of toys. First of all, the universally loved doll, of which there were many varieties. Some of them were quite crude, with no legs, or with just one imperfectly shaped arm, for example. Others were highly realistic miniatures of the human body; not only were the proportions respected but these dolls also had legs which could be moved by pulling on a set of strings. They were painted and decorated according to the taste of the manufacturer and the customer. But the brightest, gaudiest colours were reserved for the toys intended for the very small child, it being thought evidently that, in their simplicity, they would be attracted by the brilliant contrasts of bright colours.

The craftsmen who made these toys showed immense skill and attention to realistic detail: sometimes a man was figured washing, or kneading dough. Children of the upper classes sometimes had doll's houses, some of which are models,

of which an architect would have been proud. Many toys were reduced-scale imitations of every-day objects such as were used by the children's parents: tools and other implements, of both house and field, household crockery, etc.

In some instances, a Typhonian monster, or a crocodile, amused a child by its grimaces, or the motion of its opening mouth; plainly showing that children, in all ages, delight in the frightful, and play with objects which, if real, they would shudder to behold.

CIRCUMCISION

Circumcision was a rite practised by them from the earliest times. "Its origin," says Herodotus, "both among the Egyptians and Ethiopians, may be traced to the most remote antiquity; but I do not know which of those two people borrowed it from the other, though several nations derived it from Egypt during their intercourse with that country. The strongest proof of this is that all the Phœnicians who frequent Greece have lost the habit they took from Egypt of circumcising their children."

This habit probably derived from a sanitary precaution well suited to a hot climate; as always happens in such cases, the prohibition eventually assumed a sacred character, as the legislator invoked religion in order the better to ensure that the rite to which he was so attached for the benefit of the people should be properly observed.

The antiquity of its institution in Egypt is fully established by the monuments of the Upper and Lower Country, long before the Exodus and the arrival of Joseph; and Strabo tells us that "a similar rite was practised in Egypt which was customary also among the Jews." Though very generally adopted, no one was compelled to conform to this ordinance unless initiated into the mysteries or belonging to the priestly order; and it is said that Pythagoras submitted to it in order to obtain the privileges it conferred, by entitling him to a greater participation in the mysteries he sought to study.

There can be no doubt, moreover, that un-circumcised persons were commonly regarded with suspicion. They could even be associated, in the popular mind, with the class of unclean foreigners. In other words, such a person remained un-circumcised at his own risk, not to mention the added danger of having possibly displeased the gods.

As for the age at which it was proper to perform this operation, this was left to the choice of the parents. Generally, though, the fourteenth year was preferred.

That leaves the question of the instrument with which circumcision was performed.

Some have supposed that it was done by the simple implement used by Zipporah, "a sharp stone," and that certain stone knives found in the tombs of Thebes were intended for the purpose. We may conclude that the means adopted by the Egyptians were more nearly related to the "sharp knives" of Joshua than the primitive implement used by Zipporah in "the wilderness."

Left, a very realistic bas-relief...
Facing, a sovereign and his son.
Below, all the grace of adolescence.

2. PERSONAL APPEARANCE, HYGIENE AND DRESS

CLEANLINESS

The hot climate of Egypt obviously made frequent washing a matter of necessity and explains why the Egyptians regarded the use of water as a genuine pleasure. Refreshing habits of cleanliness had thus always existed amongst them; indeed they were well ahead of other peoples of the Middle East in this respect.

Egyptians felt obliged to wash before and after each meal.

This was a custom which one could not neglect without falling in the esteem of one's companions.

By way of soap the Egyptians used an absorbant with a steatite or argillaceous earth base; though not necessarily an emulsion, it was nevertheless active.

The water was poured over the bather, who kneeled or was seated on the ground. Warm as well as cold baths were used by the Egyptians, though for ordinary ablutions cold water was preferred; and both were probably recommended and taken medicinally when occasion required. In a typical scene from a tomb-painting, a lady is attended while taking her bath by four assistants, who perform various duties. One removes the jewellery and clothes she has taken off, or hangs them on a stand in the apartment; another pours water from a vase over her head, as the third rubs her arms and body with her open hands; and a fourth, seated near her, holds a sweet-scented flower to her nose, and supports her as she sits.

One readily understands the disgust they felt on seeing the squalid appearance and unrefined habits of their Asiatic neighbours, whose long beards were often the subject of ridicule to the Egyptian soldier; and for their abhorrence of the bearded and long-haired Greeks, which was so great, that, according to Herodotus, "no Egyptian of either sex would on any account kiss the lips of a Greek, make use of his knife, his spit and cauldron, or taste the meat of an animal which has been slaughtered by his hand." The same habits of cleanliness are also indicated by the "changes of raiment" given by Joseph to his brethren when they set out to bring their father to Egypt. This was clearly an attempt on their part to match the greater levels of refinement of their Egyptian neighbours.

For these reasons one can say that the barber is a product and also a living proof of civilization. The Romans, for example, like other people, first let their beards grow. It was not until 454 years after the foundation of Rome that Ticinus had barbers brought from Sicily and established the custom of shaving. Pliny tells us that Scipio the African was the first Roman to adopt the habit of daily shaving.

During mourning bathing was prohibited—a fact which suggests that the bath was viewed not merely as a necessary but also as a pleasant part of one's life. Having to do without a bath was a most disagreeable deprivation, which was viewed by the Egyptians almost as a punishment or a sign of disfavour. Even the most modest of dwellings had a bathroom of sorts; these could vary from a very simple installation all the way to the extreme refinements of the richest villas.

If the man in the street had such attitudes to cleanliness, what is there to say about the upper classes? Mania is perhaps the right word to describe the phenomenon.

As for the priests, their ablutions were astonishingly frequent: they took several complete baths every day. Apart from that they shaved their whole body, including eyelashes and eyebrows. It was the same concern for purity which inspired them to observe chastity; a healthy soul could hardly develop in a body which was not clean.

Left, toiletries: pitcher, basins and a pair of scissors. Below, even the dead were washed—a corpse being cleaned before mummification.

DRESS

Nothing was more functional than Egyptian dress, which was perfectly adapted to the climate. The most practical garments of all were obviously those of the working classes, who felt, much more than the idle rich, the harshness of the burning heat of the sun.

Among the lower classes men ordinarily wore a sort of apron or loincloth, pleated and simply knotted around the loins, the folds hanging loosely in front. Sometimes this would be accompanied by a pair of shorts reaching half-way down the thigh. And that was all. Occasionally, however, even that was felt to be too much. When doing really hard work, one could choose from two solutions: a simple piece of fabric rolled between the legs, held up, front and back, by a belt. Or, if one wished, one could wear nothing at all—perhaps the most comfortable solution of all.

The members of the upper classes also used the simple loin-cloth, but showed more sophistication and a greater sense of comfort: they wore a very full linen tunic, with broad sleeves; this garment, which was worn above the loin-cloth, reached all the way down to the ankles and provided excellent protection against the heat. Also they secured the loincloth with a more elegant belt, a sort of scarf knotted in front.

Herodotus talks of certain linen garments, with an embroidered fringe along the bottom edge, called *calasiris*. Many of these are to be seen in the bas-reliefs, though in fact they were not worn very often. He also refers to woollen cloaks, adding that it was forbidden to wear them in the temples. Cotton fabrics were, of course, known to the Egyptians, though they preferred linen. This fibre was considered to be less hot and easier to clean. It was used in the making of broad-sleeved shirts the neckline of which was closed at the neck by an adjustable string.

The dress of the priests was ritual; it consisted of a loincloth and a narrow-sleeved shirt. On top of this they used to wear a voluminous, floating robe which sometimes left the right arm free. When officiating in the temple they wore a very broad vestment attached to their belt and covering their bodies, with all due chastity, right down to the feet. Wool and leather were both forbidden materials as they derived from animals. An exception was however made in the case of a leopardskin cloak which they wore in certain ceremonies, such as the immolation of victims, water-borne processions or processions of sacred tabernacles, the presentation of offerings, or the anointing of the King. But this vestment was reserved for the

Left and below, the beautiful robe of a queen.

Middle, a royal couple walking in a garden. Rich though they may be, the garments we see here are essentially the same as those worn by everyone else.

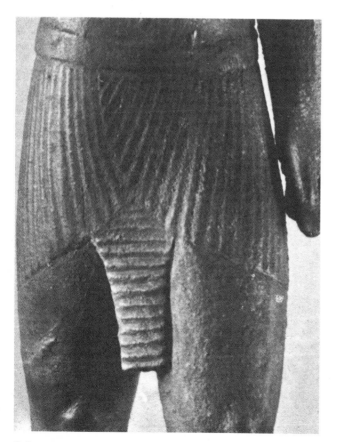

Above, a general receiving his clothes and decorations from his servants.
Below, the kind of pants which were an essential part of male attire.
Right, two types of close-fitting robes.

highest dignitaries. Moreover, this symbol was also a part of the wardrobe of the King, who used to put it on before these ceremonies were held.

It is only logical that the priests' clothes should be made of linen, which, as Plutarch observes, is perfectly consistent with the customs of men anxious to rid themselves of all natural impurities; for certainly, he adds, it would be absurd for those who take so much pains to remove hair and all other superfluities from the body, to wear clothes made of the wool or hair of animals.

The priest used to wear different emblems, depending on their rank and the ceremony which they were participating in. Here again, strict ritual had to be observed; for example, certain jewels, necklaces and bracelets had to be worn.

The true refinement of Egyptian dress, however, consisted of the art of the pleat. Pleats could be very fine, or very broad (the style known as the "sun"), or they could be divided up into large segments of fabric. The pleats were formed using fabrics which had been properly weighted with vegetable products and then carefully ironed. This was the treatment given to skirts, robes and sleeves which would have done credit to the name of a great designer.

Pleats were obviously used much more in female dress. It should be noted, moreover, that social differences were more pronounced among women—as happens in all countries. Servants, for example, often wore... a necklace and belt of pearls! And in certain cases the effect must have been

quite charming. Interestingly enough, slaves and ladies-in-waiting were not entitled to wear the same outfits as their mistresses. Frequently they wore a long narrow robe knotted at the neckline, with tight-fitting sleeves. When attending a party they used to wear a long, full robe. Subordinate rank did not, however, exclude flirtatiousness.

Women of elevated rank usually wore dresses of very soft cloth, covering them from ankles to neck. They sometimes wore richly ornate and fanciful belts. Sometimes they would leave one arm and one breast uncovered, asymmetrically. The fabrics were highly decorative, with a great variety of patterns, and bright colours. Naturally, the finest, softest and most perfect fabrics were kept specially for the use of the Queen... or the gods.

Beneath these robes they wore an underskirt of a very light and almost transparent fabric.

The costumes of the dancing girls were particularly elegant, and also notably succinct. Sometimes they consisted of a simple highly pleated loincloth, or a fairly short tunic the transparence of which suggested, rather than emphasized, the shape of the body and its choreographic movements.

Clothes were therefore quite simple, even functional, while at the same time remaining elegant. Nevertheless, the fancy was really allowed to run wild in the choice of the jewelry which went with such female attire and with which Egyptian women covered themselves literally from head to toe.

FOOTWEAR

Men and women of high rank took extraordinary care with the beauty of their sandals, this being considered an aristocratic sign of refinement. At the lower levels of society it was felt to be much more agreeable to go about barefoot. Footwear was thus a kind of social obligation, something of a nuisance, and at the same time a luxury.

The shape of the sandals varied. They were often pointed, upturned at the tip, curved like modern skates or oriental slippers. They were made with woven palm-leaves or papyrus-stalks. More rarely leather was used, often in the form of intertwined thonging.

For real style, one could line these shoes with fabric bearing the picture of a captive or an enemy; the act of permanently walking on the features of the detested person was a form of humiliation which was socially acceptable. In fact, in the hieroglyphs of the sculptures, it is not uncommon to find, after the name of a king whose courage or victories are being extolled, the words: "you have trodden on the impure Gentiles with your powerful foot".

The ancient Egyptians also had some shoes which could be tied up with laces, and also a sort of short boot, probably copied from foreign models. They were not common.

Dancers, both male and female, also preferred to go barefoot; their motions were all the lighter for it.

On certain occasions, and in the temples, the priests would remove their shoes, too; but their reasons were of quite a different nature.

devised, and that it far surpassed in comfort and coolness the modern turban.

Good-quality wigs were made of real hair. Depending on one's taste, the hair could be plaited or curled; however, a cheap solution was to use a wig made of strands of wool—dyed black, of course.

The wig was worn both out of doors and in the house. It was crowned with flowers, and garlands, and worn with pins and a sort of clip which could be made of gold, silver or precious stones. Perfume was added in abundance; and one instance occurs of a wreath of leaves placed round the crown of a king, on a statue of Sabaco, in Ethiopia, precisely similar to those worn by the Romans.

WIGS

It may seem odd that so warm a covering to the head should have been adopted in the climate of Egypt; but when we recollect that they always shaved the head, and that the reticulated texture of the groundwork on which the hair was fastened, allowed the heat of the head to escape, while the hair effectually protected if from the sun. It is evident that no better covering could have been

THE HAIR

The ancient Egyptians were remarkable for their rather special attitudes towards any sort of hair. both animal and human.

The Egyptians, says Herodotus, "only let the hair of their head and beard grow in mourning, being at all other times shaved;" which agrees perfectly with the authority of the Bible, and of the sculptures. So particular, indeed, were they on

Above and below, care of the hair. Right, a comb.

28

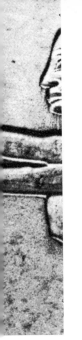

this point, that to have neglected it was a subject of reproach and ridicule; and whenever they intended to convey the idea of a man of low condition, or a slovenly person, the artists represented him with a beard. It is amusing to find that their love of caricature was not confined to the lower orders, but extended even to the king; and the negligent habits of Rameses VII are indicated in his tomb at Thebes by the appearance of his chin, blackened by an unshorn beard of two or three days' growth. But it was likewise given as the test of hardships undergone in a severe campaign; and the warlike character of Rameses the Great is pointed out in the same manner.

Among the poor, for whom wigs were an inaccessible luxury, it was not uncommon to go out bareheaded, whether or not the sun was shining. As Herodotus comments, with a smile, the Egyptian skull was apparently tougher than that of other peoples, since it was able to protect against sunstroke.

We know that certain types of hat existed in ancient Egypt, but they were not widely used, or even well thought of; indeed, they were considered as a barbarous piece of attire.

Children were also clean-shaven, with the exception of a lock on the side, in front of and at the back of the head, which they wore long and in a sort of pouch. This lock was the distinctive sign of childhood.

Of course, because of this custom, the barber was an important figure in Egyptian society, constantly in demand. His services were needed every day, and he could be seen rushing about the streets, busily at work. He never went anywhere without his little bag, containing his instruments: a small axe with a curved handle, and a number of well sharpened knives, of different sizes.

Some Egyptians, on a well-shaven chin, would wear a false beard. Its shape, however, was decreed by ritual: it had to be short and round. The long, square beard was reserved for the King. Like the lion's tail, which he secured on his person during certain royal ceremonies, it was a royal emblem. As for the pointed tapering beard, it was the attribute of the gods. No-one was authorized to wear this divine emblem during his lifetime; it could only be worn after death, and then only if the person's life had qualified him for admission to heaven, to the eternal life where one is reunited with Osiris.

We should add that while hair of any sort was viewed with some disdain, red hair was utterly detested. It was in any case rare among Egyptians, being found only as a rule on foreigners, who were well advised to cover it up with a cap or a wig, in keeping with the customs of polite society. However, if it was a native Egyptian whose head was thus lamentably covered with such a red thicket, the only possible solution was the repeated use of the razor!

FEMALE HAIR STYLES

Ladies wore their hair long and plaited. The back part was made to consist of a number of strings of hair, reaching to the bottom of the shoulder-blades, and on each side other strings of the same length descended over the breast. The hair was plaited in the triple plait, the ends being left loose: or, more usually, two or three plaits were fastened together at the extremity by woollen string of corresponding colour. Around the head was bound an ornamental fillet, fastened with a lotus bud, falling over the forehead; and the strings of hair at the sides were separated and secured with a comb or a band, ornamented in various ways according to the fancy of the wearer; and occasionally a round stud or pin was thrust into them at the front.

We shall find many such pins in the jewel-caskets

of elegant Egyptian ladies; they were made of gold or silver, enriched with precious stones and fine patterns. The ladies used combs with one or two rows of teeth. The more coquettish among them would wear an embroidered headband to keep their hair back behind their ears.

The hair-styles of ladies-in-waiting was different from that of their mistressess. They used to knot their hair behind the head in a large bun, or in numerous plaits which would then hang down at either side of the head.

These hair-styles were generally most fetching— apart from which, Egyptian women were very pretty.

JEWELRY

In order to enhance what was after all a rather simple type of apparel, Egyptians of both sexes used to wear large numbers of jewels. Their jewel-caskets were richly adorned and of the most varied shapes.

Earrings were among the commonest forms of jewelry in use amongst the ancient Egyptians. They were made of a simple gold ring, broad and flat, and of as much as 2 to 3 inches in diameter. Sometimes several rings were welded together, this being the traditional ornament worn by the dancing girls; it could be very heavy.

Left, a typical hairdo and, above, a lady of distinction readying herself for a sortie into the social life of her day: a servant adjusts her necklace.

Persons of elevated rank had rings inlaid with precious stones or wrought in the shape of a snake representing an aspic. At Thebes, rings have been found in the form of dragons or arabesques; they are highly diverse and very beautiful. Ears were pierced, and ladies had to get used to wearing such a heavy and cumbersome ornament—not always an easy matter.

Rings were very common. Women used to wear them, sometimes two or three on the same hand, or even a ring on every finger, including the thumb. The concentration of rings was usually greatest on the left hand. The ring finger was the preferred one, though this location for a ring did not have marital implications.

Most of these rings were made of gold, though silver and bronze were also used. They were of the most varied shapes. The simplest of them were decorated with variable amounts of engraving, and were more or less coiled or twisted. Many were shaped like a serpent biting its own tail. They were sometimes adorned with a more or less prominent kitten made of one of the coloured stones which occur in such abundance in Egypt. The kitten is often in the form of a seal representing a symbolic motif: for example, a scarab, the Egyptian symbol *par excellence,* or perhaps that very elongated eye, which was supposed to bring good luck. The form

31

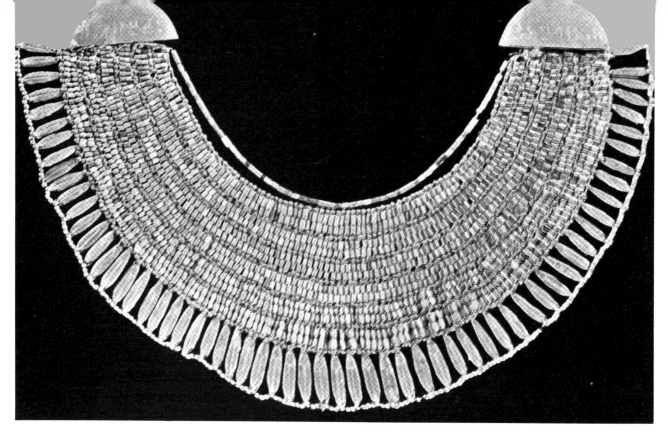

Above and right, bottom, jewelry from the early Egyptian period.

represented could be a flower, a snail or a seashell. The Egyptian imagination was fertile.

A word about semi-precious stones. The spectrum of colours in these stones is fascinating; it ranges from the limpid blue of lapis-lazuli to the turbulent blue of turquoise and the speckled gold of cornaline, these being the three stones which are most representative of the Egyptian jeweller's art. But there were also agate, amethyst, and haematite. In addition, we should note that Egyptian craftsmen worked wonders with enamel, large plaques of which were decorated with hieroglyphs or cartouches.

Less rich women were content with rings of ivory, bronze or even porcelain, all of which were very pretty. On certain rings, the stone, which was flat on both sides, turned around a gold wire secured to either end of the ring.

It is evident, therefore, that Egyptians had a great variety of rings; and the same is true of bracelets. These were worn on the arm, the wrist and even the ankle. They were very heavy, of gold, and were frequently inlaid with precious stone and articulated in the form of plates. Others were shaped like coiled cobras, their scales painstakingly rendered. It is interesting to note that men were quite as fond of them as women, and that both sexes wore them to an equal degree. One particular bracelet has been found which must certainly have been worn by the Pharaoh himself: it is made of gold.

But the main item in the vast jewel-casket was the

necklace. It was here that the imagination, taste and skill of the craftsmen expressed themselves fully. The necklace occupied an important place in Egyptian dress. From the simple gold chain, more or less thick, to the breast-plate which was so heavy and enormous that it needed a counter-balance on the back of the neck—this latter item also being a work of art—they were all truly admirable creations.

Pendants of all sorts could be hung from them: Baroque pearls, enamelled lotus flowers, sea-shells made from precious metals, chiselled flowers, acorns, stone teardrops. Plus, of course, the symbolic motifs, such as the Egyptian eye which protects one from the evil eye, the coiled *ankh*, or symbol of life, the scarab beetle holding between his hind legs the ball which symbolizes the sun, Râ the Magnificent. It should be noted that this sacred scarab which occurs in countless images in Egyptian statuary is none other than the common dung-rolling beetle, and that the symbolic ball in fact consists of decaying excrement!

Porcelain, with its gentle shades of blue, ochre or russet, was the basis for numerous ornaments, and its pearls went to make some very fragile and graceful necklaces.

As for the breast-plate, made of gold or silver, consisting of long hinged plates inlaid with gems and bordered with filigree patterns, it was often a spectacularly sumptuous item. Worn on a

The above bas-relief is entitled the "gift of gold".

simple tunic of pleated linen, and secured at the waist by a matching belt, it imparted to the appearance of the person wearing it the right degree of splendor, elegance and luxury. The royal breast-plates were of course the most beautiful, the richest and the most finely worked; they often consisted of lattice-work gold plates, for the sake of lightness, in *cloisonné,* inlaid with hieroglyphic motifs.

Even the children, who went about with nothing on the greater part of the time, wore a necklace from which a locket or an amulet was suspended. One can be seen on the chest of the god Harpocrates, the patron of youth, who is always shown with his finger in his mouth, a typical childish gesture. It was sometimes made of gold though it could be made of leather, hard stone, ivory or silver. It was often hollow, and contained a piece of papyrus bearing a magic formula. These amulets were supposed to protect those wearing them and to incite them to virtue and wisdom.

Left, assorted jewels: a breast-plate, bracelet and clip. A young woman is adjusting the earrings of the hostesses of a harem. Above, a make-up spoon, the equivalent of which is found on the lid of the casket reproduced below.

TOILETRIES

No elegant Egyptian lady did not possess her own private beauty parlour, as it were. Even since the earliest times of Egypt, it had been considered a refinement for ladies to make up their eyelids and eyebrows. Great care was needed to make the outline properly, thus enlarging the contour of the eye. Besides the fact that it emphasized the breadth and the depth of the naturally beautiful Egyptian eye, *kohl,* the substance used for this purpose, was thought to be good for the sight and an effective way of preventing eye diseases such as trachoma, conjunctivitis, and ophtalmic disorders which are endemic in hot countries.

Kohl is a powdered ointment, of varying composition. It always derives, however, from the incomplete combustion of various fatty substances: antimony, black manganese oxide or lead. It could be coloured blue or green or given a rainbow effect. It used to be kept in little vases, the simpler ones being made of painted wood, the richer specimens being of bronze or gold, inlaid or engraved with decorative patterns. It was applied with a

small stalk made to match the receptacle itself. Some of these small objects are very beautiful.

Next to them on the lady's table were ointment boxes which ranged from the most rudimentary to the most precious, and vases of alabaster, onyx or gold, used to store perfume or incense.

Perfumes were used a great deal, perhaps immoderately even, and their smell lingered on and on. They were made from walnut or olive oil and natural essences. Julius Pollux mentions a black oil, and tells us that the sagdas was used as an ointment. Theophrastus, for his part, claims that the ointments were colourless. But this divergence of opinion is easily explained: these ointments were very numerous, and varied according to both the request of the buyer and the taste of the manufacturer. Strabo notes that women of the lower classes used kikki or castor-berry oil, an oil which was more commonly used as fuel in lamps of the period. Its scent cannot have been a very distinguished one!

Essences were extracted from numerous plants, such as *simsim,* olive, almond, linen, *selgam,* rape, *seemga,* and even from vegetables such as lettuce!

The spoons used for make-up are delightful objects. Sometimes they were made in the form of an outstretched arm ending in a open hand, or the form of the body of a young girl holding a mirror. The handles of the exquisite objects are finely wrought, decorated with garlands of papyrus or lotus, coiled or engraved. The handles of mirrors were also highly elaborate. The mirrors themselves were made of polished metal.

Lastly, as we have seen, hairpins were very widely used, and were highly ornate, being inlaid with stones or finely worked metal. Curved combs were also used to secure the hair. These were of wood or metal, and had either one or two rows of teeth, big on one side and shorter on the other. The middle was carved and highly ornate. Others bore a reproduction of a little animal.

The ultimate luxury, reserved, by definition, for idle hands, was the fan. The simplest ones were made of an ordinary lotus leaf, while the richest were made of splendid ostrich feathers. Between these two, the Egyptians used a more or less ornate papyrus fan decorated with bright colours and original patterns.

Walking sticks were also used, being, *inter alia,* a sign of authority. They were between three and six feet long; they were made of wood enriched with a carved boss representing a ram, a flower or a bird's beak. This boss was sometimes made of hard stone or a semi-precious gem.

The general appearance and style of Egyptian dress withstood the passage of time; it varied very little over the centuries. This was because, being perfectly adapted to this climate, it was also very elegant: a most successful arrangement.

Left, a portable mirror.
Below, a young woman puts
on her lipstick with a brush.
Right, a perfume spoon.

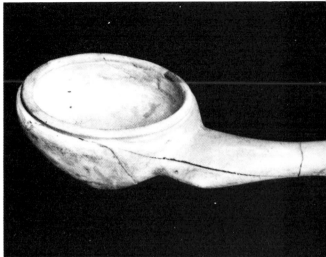

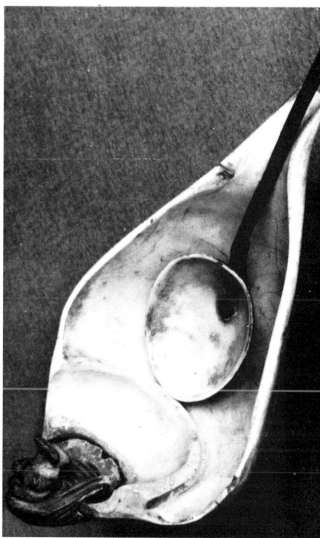

3. HOUSES AND INTERIORS

HOUSES

People living in the extremely hot and dry climate of Egypt require only the barest minimum of housing. It has been suggested, after all, that Egyptian tombs were infinitely better decorated and cared for than their houses. The brevity of man's stay on earth was a point which the priests hammered away at constantly. Yet, since the earliest times, Egyptians loved their houses.

The family dwelling developed considerably over the ages. During the neolithic period, the gradual drying of the climate of North Africa caused the disappearance of the vast equatorial forests which used to cover this region, thus obliging the inhabitants to move back to the Nile. As man progressed from a life of hunting to one of farming, he began to settle; at this point the first houses built of solid materials appeared.

The Egyptians then organized themselves in villages in the midst of cultivated land and pastures. The first villages were nothing more than huts surrounded by picket fences. Houses were also made of reeds kept taut by means of stakes embedded in the ground. They were either an enclosed oval structure, or merely a sort of reed wind-break, erected to face north or south-east.

Besides these primitive dwellings, there were also more elaborate structures. They consisted of an oval enclosure, measuring about 6 feet at its largest point, with a low wall, 2 feet high, made of an agglomerate of kneaded mud blocks mixed with grass. The ground was slightly hollowed out like a funnel, and equipped in the centre with a porous vase with a neck, buried in the earth and intended as a way of collecting water. These dwellings were about one foot lower than ground level, and the entrance often had the leg bone of a hippopotamus as a threshold. The roof was made of reeds, to which blankets or animal hides were sometimes added.

A hearth was sometimes built in the middle of the hut and a basket was sunk into the ground nearby to serve as a grain silo and a larder. Its wicker lid was plugged with clay.

Left, symbolic representation of a garden, with numerous trees and a central pond.
Right, model of a granary of the XI Dynasty.

Standards of living gradually rose; mud bricks were used according to a new technique; instead of simply piling one crudely kneaded mud brick on top of the other, they now secured a mass of mud inside a kind of reed frame where it was left to dry—a kind of ancient precursor of our reinforced concrete. Using this material, which was almost prefabricated, the Egyptians then began to build rectangular houses. The wicker baskets were replaced by earthenware jars, which were certainly more hermetically sealed.

Towns were generally surrounded by a crenellated wall made of bricks. Sometimes this wall was double.

Subsequently, houses were made of dried bricks, and they continued to be very light and not very

strong. There was no threat from the weather, however. In the labourers' villages located near the major construction sites—pyramids or tombs—the housing was always the same: two main rooms in front and two rooms at the back, one of them serving as a kitchen. It was even possible to use the roof as a terrace, accessible by a stairway.

Not far from these villages stood the huge villas of the dignitaries. Some of these, which were built to accomodate large families and a whole tribe of servants, had as many as seventy rooms, not counting the outhouses!

It was during the New Empire that private construction developed considerably. The attempt to meet both functional and aesthetic requirements was evident.

Varying in form and quality, the houses were arranged along the straight and narrow streets of the towns. All of them were made of sun-dried brick. Temples, houses, farms and palaces all used this same building material, the manufacture of which occupied thousands of workers the whole length of the Nile. The bricks were sometimes made with a mixture of straw.

The demand for these bricks was such that, despite the ease, speed and low cost of production, it became a government monopoly, and vast profits thus accrued to the coffers of the State. Unauthorized persons were simply not allowed to make bricks; and, just to make quite sure, the seal of the King or his high officials was sometimes added to the brick as it was made.

Such uniformity of construction avoided an excessive contrast between the dwellings of the different social classes. The smaller houses were of necessity built terrace-style, and formed an unbroken façade along the side of the street. They usually consisted of nothing more than a ground floor and one upstairs floor. Two upper floors were a rare sight indeed, as Egyptians did not like very tall houses.

The dwellings of the richer citizens often covered a vast surface area; in such cases the side wall or the outer enclosure ran along the side of the street.

Their plans were regular, the rooms being usually arranged round an open area, or on either side of a long passage to which an entrance court led from the street. The court was an empty space, considerably larger than the Roman *impluvium,*

probably paved with stone, or containing a few trees, a small tank, or a fountain in its centre; and sometimes, though rarely, a flight of steps led to the main entrance from outside.

It was not unusual for several houses to share a common courtyard. Only very big houses stood entirely on their own grounds; these had a surrounding wall and several entrances often opening on to several streets. All of them had a porch or a portico, that of the main entrance being the most lavishly decorated and the biggest. Such entrances were often framed between a pair of columns. A statue of the King was frequently placed nearby.

Decorative flags and ribbons were placed under the capital, and the name of the owner was often to be seen either above or to the side of the door.

A line of trees ran parallel with the front of the house; and to prevent injuries from cattle or from any accident, the stems were surrounded by a low wall, pierced with square holes to admit the air.

The height of the portico was about twelve or fifteen feet, just exceeding that of the cornice of the door, which was only raised by its threshold above the level of the ground. On either side of the main entrance was a smaller door, which stood at an equal distance between it and the side wall, and was probably intended for the servants, and those who came on business.

On entering by the porch, one passed into an open court, *aula*, or hall of the Romans, containing a *mandara*, or receiving room for visitors. This building, supported by columns, decorated with banners, was closed only at the lower part by intercolumnar panels, over which a stream of cool air was admitted, and protection from the rays of the sun was secured by an awning that covered it. On the opposite side of the court was another door, the approach to the *mandara* from the interior; and the master of the house, on the announcement of a stranger, came in that way to receive him.

The courtyard communicated with another larger yard by a central portico. In the main body of the building, the rooms were arranged symmetrically.

Both palaces and villas were studiously designed so as to escape from the heat. They were built facing away from the sun as much as possible, and they had high ceilings. Moreover, ventilation was a subject which received the greatest attention. For example, many rooms on the upper floor were equipped with a kind of wind funnel known as the *mulquf*, consisting of planks or reed mats secured to a wooden frame. It was built facing into the prevailing breeze, and thus did much to refresh the atmosphere in the room below.

On the top of the house was a terrace, which served for a place of repose as well as for exercise during the heat; since, being covered with a roof supported by columns, the sun was excluded and a refreshing stream of air passed through it. It was here, too, that they slept at night in the summer season, like the modern inhabitants of the country; and, according to Herodotus, they protected themselves from the gnats by a mosquito net, or trusted to the current of wind passing over this elevated space, to keep those troublesome insects away. However, the very fine mesh of these nets also kept in the heat. One therefore had to choose between sweating or getting bitten.

Interior decorating was always very simple—a far cry from the interiors of tombs or temples. More often than not it was reduced to friezes of birds, flowers or fruit.

The outhouses of the rich villas were built on the outside of the property, against the surrounding wall. Workshops, silos, stables. kitchens, servants' quarters and the sheds were kept well away from the master's lodgings, so that the principal occupants of the building should not have to be bothered by smells and noise. Better still, such utilitarian premises were further insulated from the rest of the property by one or more rows of trees. In this way they were less of an eyesore as well. Numerous warehouses made it possible to store the merchandise and foodstuffs which were needed by such an establishment. Wine and oil were kept in large amphoras like those used by the Romans.

The rooms and the corridors of the main house were all coated with a layer of stucco both inside and outside. As we have seen, the decor was fairly simple. The columns of the porch and corridors were coloured, and, when of wood, they were stained to represent stone; and this fondness for imitating more costly materials, as hard stone and rare woods, proves their love of show, and indicates a great advancement in the arts of civilised life.

Besides the owner's name, they sometimes wrote a lucky sentence over the entrance of the house, for a favourable omen, as the "good abode," the *mínzel mobárak* of the modern Arabs, or something similar; and the lintels and posts of the doors, in the royal mansions, were frequently covered with hieroglyphics, containing the ovals and titles of the monarch.

The windows, or perhaps one should say the

shutters, were made of solid panels closed by a bar and a bolt. They were carefully painted. All the openings were small. It seems the ancient Egyptians preferred to do without light rather than let in the heat.

The richer town-dwellers sometimes had a second residence in the country. Besides arable land on which vegetables and fruit were grown, some of these houses also had spacious ornamental gardens.

In the farms, travelling carriages and plaustra were kept in the stables or barns near the main residence. But, as we have seen, the premises where the animals were kept were situated well away from the house, though within the limits of the property. A canal bringing water from the nearest river or stream ran around the outer edge of the farm and wound its way through the garden itself.

The granaries were also apart from the house, and were enclosed within a separate wall, like the *fructuaria* of the Romans; and some of the rooms in which they housed the grain appear to have had vaulted roofs. These were filled through an aperture near the top, to which the men ascended by steps, and the grain, when wanted, was taken out from a door at the base.

The management of the houses and grounds was entrusted to stewards, who regulated the tillage of the land, received whatever was derived from the sale of the produce, supervised the returns of the quantity of cattle and stock upon the estate, settled all the accounts, and condemned the delinquent peasants to the stick, or any punishment they might deserve. To one were entrusted the affairs of the house, another supervised the cultivation of the fields; and the extent of their duties. or the number of those employed, depended on the quantity of land or the will of its owner.

So much for the villas of the rich. The dwellings of the fellahs were infinitely simpler than that, having only a single yard, with two or three lean-to sheds and a single bedroom, on the first floor, with the most rudimentary standards of comfort. All of them, however, both rich and poor, had a toilet; this was true even of the humblest shacks.

Each house had a cellar which was used to store the more perishable foodstuffs.

Efficiency was a most notable feature of all Egyptian dwellings. They were perfectly designed for a relaxed life. Here again, the practical sense of the Egyptians was paramount. The space within each house was distributed harmoniously and functionally. Naturally the great landowners lived magnificently in their vast villas; yet, the fellah's house was quite as comfortable as it might be in modern Egypt. The furnishings were designed with the same purpose in mind. However, one has to admit that house building is always much easier in a country where neither cold nor rain were to be reckoned with...

FURNITURE

During the long centuries of Pharaonic civilisation the art of furniture-making evidently evolved a great deal. Yet, though tastes and techniques may have changed, Egyptian furniture tended to

remain more or less the same. The only large items we know of are beds, armchairs and chests. This is not surprising, however, when one remembers that these are among the most practically important pieces in the house.

The art of furniture-making was seriously hampered in Egypt by the fact that the country had no precious woods of its own. Its only trees were those which provided the coarser woods used in construction. Woods for careful finishing therefore had to be imported, and were consequently rare and expensive. Even so, Egyptian cabinet-makers were truly masters of their craft and were able to produce genuine works of art. Perhaps their work was all the more refined precisely because their materials were so costly. The rarer species of timber were imported from Syria or Lebanon.

Whereas the shape of the chests varied only little over the dynasties, their decorative detail came increasingly to mask their utilitarian nature. They continued to be long and squat, and their dimensions grew. Some of them were covered with metal plates; others were inlaid with ceramics, glass, and even semi-precious stones. Certain sculpted motifs were integrated into the piece of furniture itself; they usually represent the traditional symbols: *ankh,* scarab, and the heads of animals such as the lion, jackal or vulture— in other words, nothing particularly original.

On the other hand, there was an abundance of seats of exceedingly varied shape. They were made with great care. As techniques improved, so the ornamental work evolved in an amazing quest for beauty and comfort combined. Some of the Egyptian folding chairs which have been found have very elegant birds' heads— ducks or swans— at the ends of the cross-pieces. There were also stools decorated with lattice-work patterns. There were numerous chairs, with high or low backs which were themselves highly ornate, and which, in a fine combination of comfort and harmony, could be either straight or rounded.

The armchairs were even more richly ornamented. Sometimes the whole of the lower part would be an imitation of the stylized bodies of two lions or two jackals. The same motifs were continued on the backs and armrests.

These pieces of furniture were decorated with ebony or ivory, or even gold plate. The seats were

stuffed and covered with richly coloured fabrics; or they could be made of simple leather thonging or papyrus strands, which provided a measure of sprung suspension. Much use was made of cushions, some of which were made with embroidered fabrics or animal hides, the most valued of which was that of the leopard. They were filled with either cotton of feathers.

Beds were always designed for comfort. They were usually decorated with grotesque symbolic figures: the god Bes, a nasty-looking dwarf with a lion's head who was, nevertheless, capable of driving away evil spirits, and that of the hippopotamus god, Thoueris, patron of fertility and childbirth. Unfortunately, he was none too pretty either: in fact both these figures would seem to be more conducive to nightmares than pleasant dreams, but that was apparently not the case.

The legs of the beds were often shaped like the legs of animals, with great artistry.

The pillow was replaced by the delightful Egyptian head-rest—a luxury item made of precious woods, ivory, porcelain, gold or silver, which did much, apparently, for the graceful poise of the Egyptian head. At first sight, they do not seem as comfortable as they were said to be, but it seems that their users quickly became accustomed to them.

Footrests were also commonly used. Their height varied according to that of the seat before which they were placed. Sometimes their functions were combined, when they served as a rather low stool or a rather high footrest.

Of course, there were also certain types of thrones for the use of persons of high rank, the King, the dignitaries and the higher echelons of the priesthood. These thrones were sometimes two-seaters, as in the case of that used by the host and hostess at a fashionable dinner-party. Chairs carried by porters were also reserved for the very rich or the very old.

When they did not have enough precious wood available to them, Egyptian craftsmen devised a clever solution by dressing up the poorer material, with the help of varnish, to look like a much rarer species. Paint was also used, but with less success.

Some people had neither seats nor even cushions; all that was left in such cases was the exceedingly ordinary reed mat. Each household had a number of these, which were used in the squatting

position so frequently seen in the sculptures.

Although tables were rare and not very much in demand, the Egyptians did have them.

The Egyptian tables were round, square, or oblong; the former were generally used during their dinners, and consisted of a circular flat summit, supported, like the *monopodium* of the Romans, on a single shaft or leg in the centre, or by the figure of a man, intended to represent a captive. Large tables had usually three or four legs, but some were made with solid sides; and though generally of wood, many were of metal or stone; needless to say, they were not easy to move about.

The most superb Egyptian furniture which has come down to us is that which was locked away in the tomb of Tutankhamen. It even betrays an excessive fondness for outrageously overloaded ornamentation of a highly pretentious nature, with a heavy insistence on ritual symbolism. Even so, one has to recognize the sheer merit of the craftsmanship. The throne is entirely plated in gold; its feet represent the bodies of two lions whose heads are in repoussé gold. The back and the armrests are inlaid with ceramics and multi-coloured stones forming a delightful image of the young king and his queen. All the official splendour and the glorification of the monarch seem to fade away, however, to leave only the charm of an intimate family scene.

The tomb of this young king also contains a remarkable chest, made of cedar and bearing the seal of the Pharaoh. The symbol of life, *ankh*, and some divine sceptres, symbolizing wealth, are represented in a lattice-work design.

A much smaller casket has a number of admirable hunting scenes, in which the King is seen standing majestically in his chariot, towering over frightened lions, his enemies, who are transfixed with arrows, and a number of galloping horses.

These are truly remarkable items, testifying to an art which is not to be found in the normal furniture of the ancient Egyptians; on the whole, however, their furniture was practical and artfully done.

It is therefore evident that Egyptians spent much time and money on the improvement of their abodes.

Two sorts of crockery were in use: one for more ordinary purposes, and the other for special occasions. The ordinary variety was made of pottery

A garden, trees,
a lotus flower
being watered...
A person kneeling
beneath a
palm-tree quenching
his thirst
from a stream.

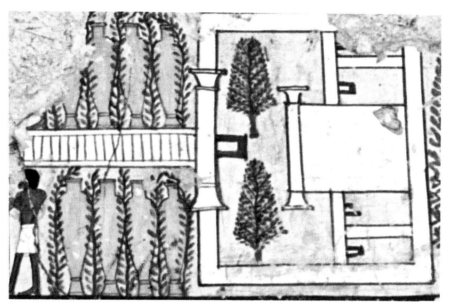

This trunk with shafts (XIV century BC) is made of wood inlaid with ivory, bronze and gold.

and was not particularly pretty. The second kind, however, was made of stone: blue or black shale, granite or alabaster. Glasses, cups and goblets were cut out of rock crystal.

Household crockery considered of a number of objects: plates, dishes, soup bowls, vases, goblets, etc.

The highest refinement was represented by a superb gold service, more particularly that reserved for use in the temples, which consisted of items such as vases, ewers and kettles, most of which were marvellous works of art.

Egyptians loved flowers — a fact which accounts for the vast number of vases to be found in their houses. They were made of a variety of materials, earthenware, metal or stone. Their necks also varied, from broad and flared to tall and narrow.

Flowers livened up the interior of Egyptian houses; sometimes the walls were decorated with floral patterns. Incense and resin were burnt for their aroma and also to repel the insects, rats and lizards which tended to wander in freely through the open doors.

There can be no doubt that Egyptians loved their houses, that they kept them up well and that they decorated them to the extent they could afford. In a sense they could be said to be indoor people.

Above, armchair of the Theban period, and folding chair.
Below, stool with convex seat and frame of a bed.

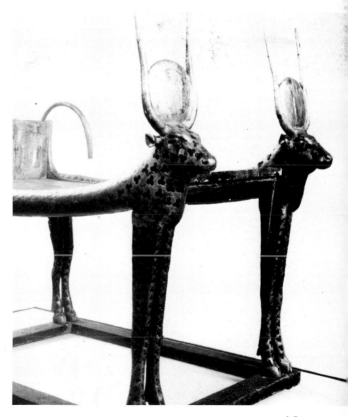

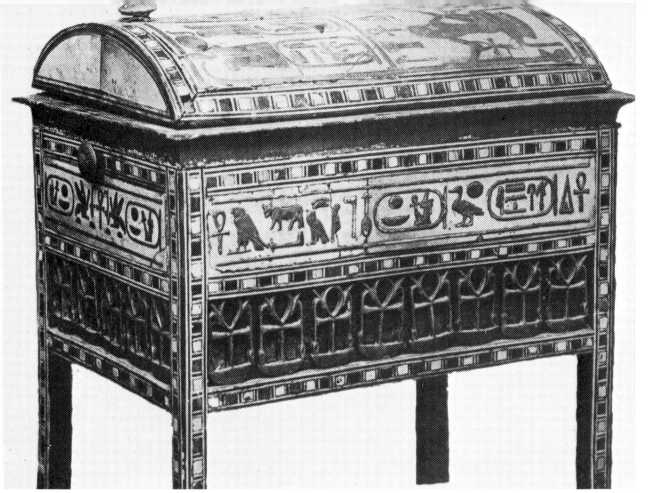

Chests, seat, furniture of a bedroom, and making the bed.

4. FOOD

THE GASTRONOMIC ART

The eating habits of the Egyptians did not remain the same throughout their long history; it seems that, at quite an early stage, their original simplicity gave way to a more sophisticated approach to cooking. At the beginning of the time of the Pharaohs, the influence of the priests managed to impose a degree of moderation and virtuous frugality; but Diodorus of Sicily and Plutarch both describe the upper classes during the reign of Menes I as indulging in excesses of gluttony and drunkenness.

At any rate, such is the reputation of the Egyptians. Shortly after the conquest of Egypt by the Persians and the accession to power of the Ptolemies, contemporary writers describe them as a debauched people given to excesses of indulgence and immoderately fond of the pleasures of food and drink. It is thought that they even used aperitive essences or stimulants, including raw cabbage, so as to be able to absorb ever greater quantities of food.

The question still remains, however: were they gluttons or gourmets? After all, surely even the mere ability to eat and drink well is in itself a sign of advanced civilisation?

MEATS AND VEGETABLES

Egypt is certainly not well endowed with grazing land. The irrigated land is just a narrow strip devoted principally to the growing of grains and vegetables. For this reason, it never had a vast amount of livestock. The Pharaohs thus took the decision—a wise one, as it later turned out—to decree that the cow was a sacred animal.

Moreover, Nout, the kindly goddess of abundance, was turned into a cow by her father Noun, and it was only right that this should be so. Thanks to this taboo, beef was subject to strict regulations, and this limitation on consumption made a constant supply possible. Extreme shortages were relatively unknown, but this was a rare dish, and

The scenes of offering reproduced on these two pages show the abundance and variety of the food available to the ancient Egyptians.

one which was always a treat for the Egyptian palate.

Goat meat, on the other hand, did appear on the Egyptian table in greater quantities; this was only logical, as goats were cheaper to raise. Mutton and lamb were not held in high esteem. Plutarch tells us that "no Egyptian eats mutton, except the Lycopolites." Allowing for the historian's exaggeration, it is nonetheless true that it was not a popular dish in such a hot climate; it sometimes came to have a peculiar taste known as the "wool taste".

The richer classes showed a distinct preference for ibex, or wild goat, the oryx, gazelle and other game animals with delicious meat. Another favourite of theirs was the plump wild goose, which was also an important part of the meat diet of the peasantry. These birds were both enormous and easy to hunt; they could even be domesticated and fattened specially for the pot. At dinner-parties large numbers of them would be slaughtered on the spot; in fact, many rich households had a special servant to do this job. Other wild birds were also hunted for their meat: quails, ducks, snipe.

And, of course, the waters of the life-giving Nile were full of fish. People used to eat this fish, though not with great enthusiasm. Yet it was a basic foodstuff, both substantial and nutritious, easy to come by, with little or no expense. The Egyptians, however, looked on fish with suspicion, perhaps because the great heat of Egypt made it difficult to keep it for any length of time, and it spoiled quickly.

In slaughtering for the table, it was customary to take the ox, or whatever animal had been chosen for the occasion, into a courtyard near the house, shortly before the meal was to take place, to tie its four legs together, and then to throw it upon the ground; in which position it was held by one or more persons, while the butcher, sharpening his broad knife upon a steel attached to his apron, proceeded to cut the throat as nearly as possible from one ear to the other, sometimes continuing the opening downwards along the throat. The blood was frequently received in a vase or basin for the purpose of cookery.

The head was left with the skin and horns, and was sometimes given away to a poor person as a reward for holding the walking-sticks of those guests who came on foot, it generally being considered as beneath the dignity of an Egyptian

to eat this part of the animal at all.

In later times, when the Greeks were settled in the country, it was sold to them, or to other foreigners: but it was frequently taken to the kitchen with the other joints; and, notwithstanding the positive assertion of Herodotus, we find that even in the temples themselves it was admitted at a sacrifice, and placed with other offerings on the altars of the gods. Yet it was not felt to be a very good sacrifice. As food, it was viewed with such disdain that no Egyptian with any self-respect would ever offer it to his guests.

Having discarded this inferior part of the carcass, the butcher would then cut up the rest with great care, starting with the feet and the neck. Each piece was cut in an order specially prescribed by tradition, so that it is very difficult to identify the parts of the animal in the drawings which represent them. At most, one can just make out the shoulder, the ham, the rump, the ribs, and, of course, the heart and kidneys. The other parts are too finely cut to permit of recognition.

Servants then carried all these pieces of meat on large wooden trays to the nearby kitchens, where they were to be prepared in various ways.

In few countries were vegetables more numerous than in Egypt; and the authority of ancient writers, the sculptures, and the number of persons employed in selling them at Alexandria, sufficiently

attest this fact. Pliny observes that the valley of the Nile "surpassed every other country in the abundance and spontaneous growth of those herbs which most people are in the habit of using as food, especially the Egyptians"; and at the time of the Arab invasion, when Alexandria was taken by Amer, the lieutenant of the Caliph Omer, no less than 4000 persons were engaged in selling vegetables in that city.

Although it is difficult to agree with Pliny when he says that they used to grow wild, one has to admit that vegetables did grow easily in Egypt, and were easily picked after the flood waters had receded; they needed virtually no attention at all. Their flavour, after such vast amounts of water and sun, was particularly agreeable. The common people derived the bulk of their diet from the abundance of vegetables, and usually reserved rare and expensive meat for special festive occasions. Herodotus tells us that the workers employed in building the pyramids consumed a vast amount of "*raphanus* or *figl*, onions and garlic". According to Strabo there was an abundance of lentils. These were grown extensively along large plots of land close to the Nile, as they fared very well in wet soil; lentils were moreover the basic staple of the diet of the lower classes throughout the time of the Pharaohs. They are nourishing, scented and keep well. Cheapness, of course, was their crowning merit.

Many other vegetables, various ill-defined roots and a large number of gourd-type vegetables such as cucumbers, melons, water-melons and pumpkins, were also part of the standard diet. Diodorus says that children had merely "a little meal of the coarsest kind, the pith of the papyrus, baked under the ashes, and the roots and stalks of marshweeds."

Put in such terms, of course, it sounds very frugal indeed; but there are roots and roots, stalks and stalks, some of which were coarse while others were real delicacies.

All these vegetables and particularly the lentils, in the form of gruel, are still to be found on the table of the fellah of today. Indeed, even the names of these foods are often the same in modern Arabic, for example, *kus*, gourd, *busl*, onion, or *tôm*, garlic.

The palm grew wild in the Nile valley, and provided an abundant, nutritious crop of dates, which required little or no care. This fruit constituted a principal part of their food, both in the month of August, when it was gathered fresh from the trees, and at other seasons of the year, when it was used in a preserved state. They had two different modes of keeping the dates; one was by the simple process of drying them, the other was by marking them into a conserve. This could be eaten either on its own, like a jam, or as an ingredient in the making of pastries.

THE KITCHEN

In the preparation of these dishes, the chef had various assistants and knew large numbers of recipes. His was an esteemed profession, and the richer families used to vie with one another to secure the services of the best chefs.

Kitchen equipment was not highly advanced. The ovens, for example, were mobile devices made of earthenware. They were cylindrical and stood about 3 feet tall. The lower part was equipped with a door through which the ashes could be removed and which allowed air to flow over the hearth, which consisted of a grill or a number of closely spaced bars.

When they did not have such an oven, cooks used to manage with a fire surrounded by three stones.

Egyptian kitchens must have been smoky places, as there were no chimneys. The draught passing over the flame cannot have been very strong, either; it is perhaps this fact which accounts for the use of numerous servants whose sole job was to keep the fire going with the help of big fans.

The chef worked on a wooden bench, either standing or crouching—in this latter case, the tray must have been down quite low. He was surrounded by numerous pots, skewers and dishes, as well as various sorts of ladles and hooks on long handles.

Meat was usually boiled in large caldrons, carefully watched over by the servant who was fanning the flames and by another whose job it was to stir the stock pot and the froth. A third servant mixed the salt, pepper and the numerous spices in a mortar; many kinds of liquids, wine, water, oil, beer and vinegar were also placed near the chef, to be poured into the pot. The ingredients were arranged on large trays hanging from the ceiling on strings—a wise precaution against the perpetual uninvited guests, such as rats and other vermin.

Besides boiling, meat, particularly venison, could be braised gently over a low flame in certain other smaller receptacles. Sticks of firewood were also used for this type of cooking, but, for roasting, charcoal pieces were spread out on a metal base which is exactly the same shape as the *magoor* still in use in Egypt today. In this way the heat penetrated more quickly and the meat remains tender. Roasts were cut into small squares which were then skewered.

Poultry was generally served whole, without the legs and the tips of the wings, though these parts were also boiled or roasted. A herb and spice stuffing was used to fill the carcass. The fat produced during the cooking of geese was carefully collected and used in the preparation of other dishes.

Fish were simmered and then dipped in fat; only the tail and fins were removed. The scales were left on and the guests themselves had to

Left, offerings of flowers, grapes and dates.
Facing, offerings of poultry and fish.
Above, offerings of fruit.

remove the bones.

For all these dishes great care was taken with the seasoning, which was both abundant and varied. Spices were used lavishly: garlic, onions, kamôon, simsim, cumin, etc. Besides beer and wine, milk was also used in cooking.

On the whole, Egyptian cooking was both healthy and pleasant to the taste.

BREAD AND PASTRIES

Egyptians loved sweet things, including pastries. In any house of note, a corps of pastry cooks and bakers displayed their talents and imagination all year long. These were quite apart from the cooks, with whom their relations were not always of the best. The frescoes show vast kitchens in which a whole army of pastry cooks are mixing wheat flour, while kneading the dough... with their feet, in large flat jars placed on the ground. This gives one

59

some idea of the vast quantity of pastry consumed!

Others were busy at large tables on which the dough was cut up into varied shapes, rolled, or sprinkled with cumin seed or the seed of the *nigella sativa*. Aromatic oils, preserves, fruit and honey were also used for this purpose.

The pieces of dough were then laid on large metallic plates and placed over the fire.

At least one servant was needed to keep the fire going and maintain its temperature, and two others to watch over the cakes, turn them over with two pointed sticks so that they would be done on both sides, and then arrange them artistically on the serving trays.

There was an endless variety of cakes, for all tastes. Some were shaped like long macaronis which had to be cut when served, while others were in the shape of animals: a recumbent ox, goat or game bird. On certain others it was customary to draw figures. The prettiest of them bristled with pointed beaks. They could also be garnished, after baking, with fresh or dried fruit. On the whole they were very sweet, and thus made a substantial meal.

As for bread, it was very widely used and highly thought of; apart from anything else, we should not forget that it replaced the fork and, almost, the spoon. In rich households the bread was white, and

made with wheat flour. The less privileged used barley and sorghum. It was baked in thin flat and rather brittle biscuit-shapes, or in thick, soft loaves. Baking was always of a very high standard. The Egyptians loved to have their bread fresh every day.

Grain was often milled in the house itself, so that miller and baker worked side by side. The flour was sifted several times until it was pure and fine. This operation was repeated daily, because none but the freshest flour was used. The dough was baked in pre-heated moulds. The fine biscuit-shapes were baked by being exposed on the sand when the sun's heat was at its greatest.

The amount of bread placed on the votive tables was quite impressive.

AT TABLE

The arrangement of the table was not left to chance. There were distinct rules of etiquette; and, even if there were no masters of ceremonies at banquets or receptions, the master or mistress of the house took in hand the smooth running of the evening.

At an Egyptian party, the men and women were frequently entertained separately, in a different part of the same room, at the upper end of which the master and mistress of the house sat close together on two chairs, or on a large armchair: the separation of the sexes was not intended as a kind of official segregation: instead, it was felt that the conversation, being about different subjects in either case, would be livelier that way.

The master and mistress of the house would rise to greet their guests and usher them into the room. Invitations were issued to both lunch and dinner. Each guest would sit at his appointed place, on a chair or a stool, or a simple cushion, or perhaps... on the floor, as the case may be. Some dinner parties were very large indeed. The guests sometimes came with their pets—dogs, cats or monkeys, who remained at their feet during the meal.

During such receptions, the pleasures of the table were always accompanied by other sorts of entertainment, in the form of a floor-show. The musicians and dancers would bow before the guests. We know that this part of the evening's fun was always very popular.

The two figures on this page represent: the first, a woman eating a duck (whole!) and the other, the decorative work on a dish.

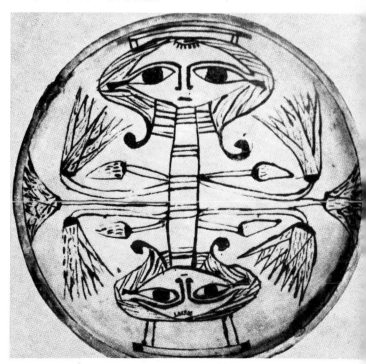

The table itself was quite rudimentary, and in no sense a fine piece of furniture in its own right. It was hardly a table at all, but merely a kind of round tray on which dishes could be put. Sometimes, as in Rome, the table was brought in by the servants fully laden, and then taken away again after dinner. More often than not, however, the dishes were brought in separately—and there were many of them: several dishes of roasted or boiled meat, poultry, fish, numerous vegetables, dairy products, fresh cheeses, and, at the end, fruit and pastries which were, as we have seen, varied and of high quality.

Table-cloths and napkins were not used, and each guest helped himself directly out of his plate. Without knives, forks or even sticks, in the Chinese style, the guests had to used their fingers to secure the morsels of food for their own consumption. It was considered stylish to use only three fingers, and only of the right hand. The guests often used bread to mop up the sauces. Yet they were entitled to a spoon, which was more or less concave, when soup was served. These soups were usually very thick and made from a lentil base.

Whenever the drinks were passed around and after the guests had drunk, a serving girl would offer them a napkin to wipe their mouths—something like the *mahrama* still in use in the Middle East.

As we have seen, before and after each meal, ablutions were performed. The servants would hold large metal basins for this purpose.

DRINK

No good table was complete without equally good drink. Grapes grew in abundance in the blessed land of Egypt, and the Egyptians were therefore no strangers to the art of wine-making.

Wine was not merely liked, it was held in high esteem. Much ceremonial surrounded the act of serving it at table—the ritual varying according to the sex of the guests. Special servants, usually under the chief female servant, were in charge of serving the wine. She was a white slave, and had a black assistant. The former carried the vase containing the precious beverage, and the second the vase which was to be filled. Female guests had their cup brought to them already full—in fact, a whole ritual had to be observed.

Wine was kept in large jars on which the origin and date were duly recorded. It was drawn off regularly so that it would not turn sour; sometimes it was boiled.

If the Egyptians treated their wine with such respect it was for one very good reason: its quality. The Greek authors of Antiquity were enthusiastic about it. There were several major growths.

Mareotis was the most esteemed, and was available in the greatest quantity. Its superiority over other Egyptian wines may readily be accounted for, when we consider the nature of the soil in that district; being principally composed of gravel, which, lying beyond the reach of the alluvial deposit, was free from the rich and tenacious mud usually met with in the valley of the Nile, so little suited for the culture of delicate wines.

According to Athenæus, "the Mareotic grape was remarkable for its sweetness", and the wine is thus described by him: "Its colour is white, its quality excellent, and it is sweet and light, with a fragrant *bouquet;* it is by no means astringent, nor does it affect the head." But it was not for its flavour alone that this wine was esteemed, and Strabo ascribes to it the additional merit of keeping to a great age.

"Still, however," says Athenæus, "it is inferior

Above, the manufacture of beer, a drink which was very common in ancient Egypt.

to the Teniotic, a wine which receives its name from a place called Tenia, where it is produced. Its colour is pale and white, and there is such a degree of richness in it, that when mixed with water it seems gradually to be diluted, much in the same way as Attic honey when a liquid is poured into it: and besides the agreeable flavour of the wine, its fragrance is so delightful as to render it perfectly aromatic, and it has the property of being slightly astringent."

Even if not all the wines of Egypt were as tasty as these, all of the hillsides near the Nile produce very pleasant wines: the wines of Anthylla, and Sebenytica which so impressed Pliny, together with the wines of the Coptic regions, and many others.

The abundance of the grape harvest was matched by the quantity of consumption. The Egyptians did not deny themselves the pleasures of this intoxicating drink. So much so that during the time of Herodotus, the country's output was no longer sufficient, and large quantities had to be imported from Phoenicia and Greece, twice a year. This wine was transported in large jars which, when emptied of their delectable contents, were put to quite another use: they were assembled at Memphis and there filled with the very high-quality water of the region, after which they were sent off to the area near the Syrian border—a sad state of affairs, to be sure. It just happens that, in some parts of the world, water is sometimes rarer than wine!

Wine was thus expensive, and the poor could

taste it only on special festive occasions and during certain ceremonies. Yet they too were fond of alcoholic beverages—the difference being that they tended to use beer.

The Egyptian beer was made from barley; but, as hops were unknown, they were obliged to have recourse to other plants, in order to give it the right flavour; and the lupin, the skirret, and the root of an Assyrian plant were used by them for that purpose. Even though Egyptians were proud of their beer, it did not really amount to much of a drink, having little sparkle and a dull taste. Its one merit was that it contained alcohol; it was drunk, at any rate, in great quantities.

In other words, if one is to believe the sculptures and the paintings in which scenes of daily life are shown, the Egyptians of both sexes were fond of eating and drinking; despite the exhortations of their priests in favour of temperance, they did occasionally drink too much, even to the point of being quite unable to stagger home. The most undignified brawls were apparently quite common. Sometimes they had to be carried home by their servants or deposited, by those same servants, with more or less decorum, in their carriages.

GRACE BEFORE MEALS

We know that this scrupulously religious people were never remiss in showing their gratitude for the blessings they enjoyed, and in returning thanks

64

to the gods for that peculiar protection they were thought to extend to them and to their country, above all the nations of the earth. It cannot, therefore, be supposed that they would have omitted a similar acknowledgement before and after meals; particularly when they were about to sit down to a nice meal. But on this point there is no need of conjecture: Josephus expressly states that the custom of saying grace before meals was practised by the Egyptians; and when the seventy-two elders were invited by Ptolemy Philadelphus to sup at the palace, Nicanor requested Eleazar to say grace for his countrymen, instead of those Egyptians who performed that duty on other occasions.

The priests encouraged this attitude, as part of their general policy of keeping the faithful constantly in mind of their religious duties. This custom was generally followed at all levels of society, and even in the Palace.

LEST WE FORGET...

During all meals, the master of the house used to keep next to him a statuette, usually of wood, about 1 1/2 to 3 feet high, of Osiris, the god who was the protector of the dead. It was in the shape of a human mummy, either standing in a sarcophagus or stretched out, as Plutarch observes, in a sort of litter.

The death of Osiris symbolized the annual drying out of the fields, now hard and barren, and their miraculous resurrection during the life-giving Nile flood.

This statuette was shown to each guest as a way of reminding him that he was mortal, that the pleasures of this world were fleeting and that he would eventually be just like that mummy.

Just as the host was about to offer his guests the most sophisticated material satisfaction and pleasure, he heeded the recommandations of the Church by inviting his guests to abide by the rules of morality and decorum, and reminded them of the fragility of all human life.

The fact is that the priests, having realized that they could not, in any case, prevent men from indulging in the satisfactions if the senses, tried at least to limit their effect by reminding everyone of the sadness and the necessities of life, and the inevitability of approaching death.

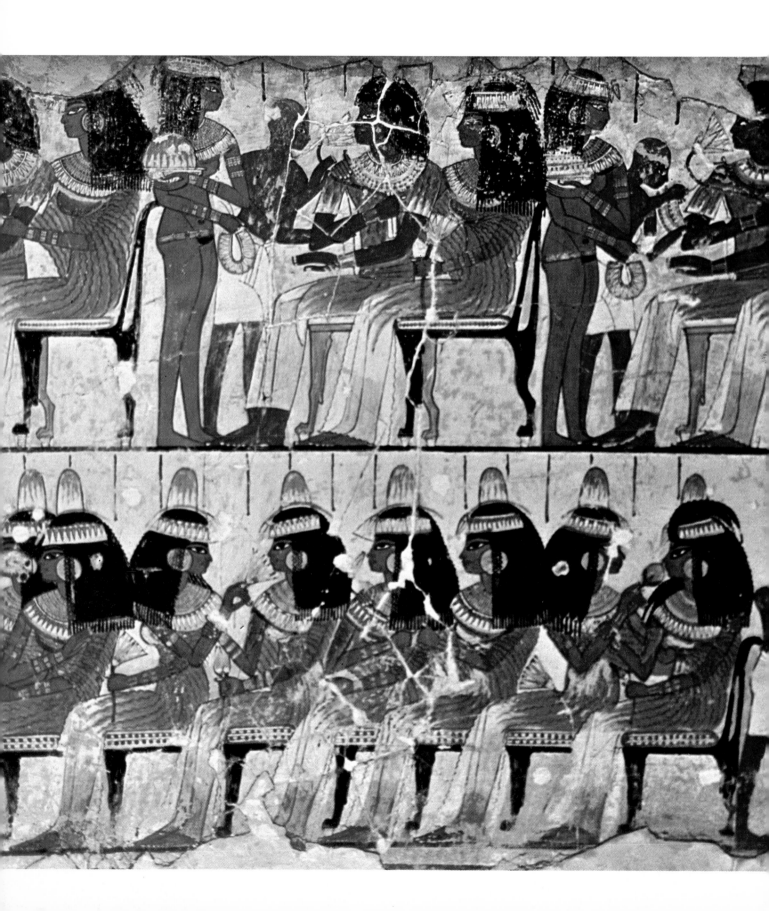

5. SOCIAL LIFE AND ENTERTAINMENTS

A RECEPTION

Being both gluttons and sophisticates at the same time, the Egyptians knew how to combine the pleasures of the palate with those of art and entertainment. No party worthy of the name was not accompanied by some sort of show and other fun and games. The menu, itself very elaborate, was thus further enhanced by music, dancing and in some instances theatrical performances, with mimes, jugglers, singers and clowns appearing in turn before the guests. All dinner-parties were thus the occasion for lavish food and equally lavish entertainment in which the Egyptians took justifiable pride.

And it was no laughing matter: preparations for a banquet would keep dozens of people busy for days on end, throughout the entire house. The majordomo was in charge of purchases, on the orders of the mistress of the house; the chef was tense and excited, constantly urging on his fearful assistants, as animals were slaughtered for table, their meat was sliced up, cooked, seasoned, tasted and arranged on the plates...

Meanwhile, in the cellar, wine was taken from the great jars, duly selected according to place of origin, the frequency with which it had been previously drawn off, the year, etc. The water was placed under running fountains to cool it; the fruit was erected artistically in the form of domes in large fruit-dishes of gold or alabaster.

The serving-girls busied themselves about the reception rooms, washing, polishing and rubbing. They took out the special dinner services from the chests where they were kept, arranged vast quantities of flowers in vases to decorate the rooms, while setting aside those which were to be distributed to the guests. Lastly, the rooms were abundantly perfumed.

Depending on whether they lived near or far away, the guests arrived in carriages, palanquins or on foot. In the latter case they walked under a parasol carried by a servant, which was made of leather stretched over a light frame. A number of other servants would walk alongside as an escort, one carrying writing tablets, another a small box, a third, when his master arrived by carriage, a footstool on which he could dismount; a lackey ran ahead to announce the arrival of his master, so that he should be welcomed in a manner befitting his rank. Naturally, this runner would have taken his sandals off, for greater ease and comfort.

The order of arrival was always governed by tacit rules of etiquette. It was considered in poor taste for a relatively unimportant man to keep people waiting; but a high dignitary would take care to arrive last, thus emphasizing his social rank.

The hosts, husband and wife, would rise each time a new guest came in and would go to the door to meet distinguished guests, and slightly less far for close friends. Endless exchanges of greetings, fulsome compliments and good wishes took place. After the initial greetings, the guests were shown into the reception room, where they were able to wash their hands and feet in elegant basins.

often made of precious metals, which were offered to them by serving girls. As soon as these ablutions were completed, the guests sat down, often with the men and the women on different sides of the room. This was not an absolute rule, however, but rather a matter of personal convenience, so that the conversation would be livelier.

THE CUSTOM OF ANOINTING

Before the beginning of the festivities and the meal itself, and in keeping with a custom which spread to Greece, a servant anointed the head of each guest, as a token of welcome. The female servants took a highly scented ointment from enormous alabaster or porcelain vases. They shaped it into a small cone, which they then carefully placed on the guests' hair—or should we say, wig—between the diadems and the crowns.

This ointment was so highly perfumed that the smell is thought to have lasted several years! The masters of the house, their children and all the servants also wore a similar cone, without, apparently, allowing them to fall off. It must have been quite a strain, but, on the other hand, it did neutralize the kitchen smells.

The custom of anointing was not confined to the appointment of kings and priest to the sacred offices they held: it was the ordinary token of welcome to guests in every party at the house of a friend.

Once they had been anointed with the "oil of joy", the guests were relieved of their shoes—which they had, in any case, put on only for the sake of elegance.

Then they were offered a flower, usually a lotus flower, or a necklace or diadem of flowers. The offering of perfume and flowers was a compulsory part of the hospitality. The room was lavishly decked out with flowers. In fact, there were special columns, of varying shape, size and height, specially for this purpose. If, by some mischance, there were no flowers, the hosts resigned themselves, as Pliny observes, to offering artificial flowers.

Diodorus informs us that when the Egyptians approached the place of divine worship, they held the flower of the *agrostis* in their hand, intimating that man proceeded from a well-watered or marshy land, and that he required a moist rather than a dry food; and it is not improbable that the reason of the great preference given to the lotus, on these occasions, was derived from the same notion. This pretty custom was also observed by the Romans and the Greeks. Like the Romans, the Egyptians sometimes scented the room with myrrh and incense. But the Lacedemonians regarded this as an effeminate habit; a striking instance is recorded by Plutarch, at the reception of Agesilaus by Tachos. A sumptuous dinner was prepared for the Spartan prince, consisting, as usual, of beef, goose, and other Egyptian dishes; he was crowned with garlands of papyrus, and received with every token of welcome; but when he refused "the sweetmeats, confections, and perfumes", the Egyptians held him in great contempt, as a person unaccustomed to, and unworthy of, the manners of civilised society.

When one was received in this way by one's friends, it was usual to take great care with one's appearance, to wear gay colours, to arrange the pleats and other folds of one's garments elegantly,

68

and to bring out one's best jewels: diadems, chokers, bracelets and rings. However, no special form of dress was prescribed for such occasions.

DRINKS BEFORE DINNER

Once they were seated, on a chair, stool, cushions, or in a armchair, the guests were offered their first glass of wine, one particularly chosen for its aperitive qualities. The Greeks found this custom the very depths of depravity: as if the Egyptians did not already eat too much, they had to stimulate their appetite even further!

The ladies received this wine in a small vessel from which it was poured, in their presence, into a cup. It was served directly to the men in a goblet with handles.

These goblets were made of gold, silver or rock crystal. Some were of copper or bronze, but all of them were elegantly made, with discernment and good taste. A special cup, often of porcelain, was reserved for the master of the house.

The great attention paid to this object from the dinner-service was an expression of the Egyptians' wish to honour their guests in every possible way.

They had no *rex convivi,* the Roman master of ceremonies whose job it was to ensure everyone was having a good time and that no excesses were committed. But the master of the house proposed the numerous—sometimes *excessively* numerous—toasts himself. Temperance was certainly not one of the major virtues of the ancient Egyptians!

ENTERTAINMENT

While awaiting the arrival of the remainder of the guests, and for the pleasure of all present, musicians performed. They had been hired long in advance, as soon as the party was first arranged. They were carefully chosen. There were several instruments—harp and lyre, guitar, for the strings, and numerous flutes and pipes, for the winds; there was also percussion, drums and tambourines—all under the direction of a conductor.

The musicians played and sang before, during and after the meal. After dinner they were joined by a new troupe, including dancers, male and female, mimes and jugglers.

A feature common to the stele reproduced on the left and the mural painting from Thebes shown above: the people shown are holding lotus flowers in their hands and apparently enjoying their perfume.

The jugglers, who were extremely clever, worked essentially with balls, though they clowned around also, seeking to outwit each other in skill and buffoonery. They made the audience laugh just by their appearance: they were dressed in ridiculous pointed bonnets with grotesque garlands and ribbons.

They also kept up a steady banter designed to amuse the guests; but they took good care to stay within the bounds of discretion and decency. The limits of propriety must not be exceeded, as the master of the house insisted, above all else, on ensuring that his guests were content and relaxed, and in no way embarrassed or offended.

Trained animals sometimes joined in the entertainments. The Egyptians loved to domesticate animals, particularly dogs. They treated them very well and showed them every consideration.

The death of a pet caused every member of the household to go into mourning. Everyone had to shave his eyebrows after the death of a pet cat. In the case of a dog, it was much worse: the whole body had to be shaved. Pets were often embalmed and buried with every conceivable care. Herodotus relates many anecdotes about the love of the Egyptians for their pets.

He quotes the case of a Roman who, one day, accidentally killed a cat and came close to being lynched by a furious mob for it!

"Training" is perhaps not the right word to describe the relations between the Egyptians and their dogs. "Domestication" is more appropriate; in any case, this was one of the major pastimes of the entire people of Egypt.

Dogs were treated everywhere as the companion and helpmate of their masters. At banquets such as the one we have described, it was not unusual for a good half of the guests to come with their favourite pet. Close on the heels of arriving guests, one might see an Arabian gazelle-hound, a greyhound or a basset-hound. All of them would have their own name. Cats or monkeys could be brought with one, too; as we shall see, the monkey was intended to amuse, but cats were a favourite pet of the Egyptians in any case.

In the remote past the cat had been wild, but it later became tamer as it rose in the esteem of its human hosts: it wore a collar, and could be led around on a lead. With proper instruction, however, cats could be a valuable helpmate for their masters when out hunting. Yet they could also learn to live peaceably with domesticated game birds. It was not unknown for a goose to follow the children of the household and act as a guardian.

Trained dogs often performed with clowns and jesters: they were made to do tricks and balancing acts, they could be dressed up or taught to pull a small carriage.

As for monkeys, they could make everybody laugh with their antics. They would come on dressed up in jewels, with a wig. They could even be taught to play various instruments, such as tambourines or cymbals, so well that they merited the applause of the dinner guests. Generally they got on well with the cats and dogs, but not so well with the geese, which were quite aggressive. These monkeys were very alert and thus able to dodge away from their attackers.

Besides the animals which were invited with their masters, there were others, therefore, who were there solely to perform; yet the atmosphere between the two groups remained placid.

This fondness for animals went hand in hand with a very special devotion to the sacred animals, of which there were many. They included the sacred bull Apis, the ram of Amon, the falcon of Horus, the dog of Anubis, the cat of Bastet and also the crocodile of Sebek and many others.

This entire troupe therefore entertained the assembled party throughout the evening. And then they moved on to other houses, to entertain at other receptions. Sometimes they performed in the streets, to the joyous approval of the passers-by.

Performing artists were not a highly esteemed social group. Their number sometimes included a few slaves; but their talents were certainly appreciated.

AFTER-DINNER MERRYMAKING

Besides the floor-show thus put on for the benefit of the guests, they could also amuse themselves in a number of other more active ways, instead of merely being spectators.

At all parties a number of amateurs would get up and perform wild dances; their choreography may not have been the most professional, but their capers and antics, accompanied by clapping of hands, were highly amusing. With one's shoes off, one came to feel quite light-headed, and, with the help of a glass of wine, the oppressive weight of the heat could almost be forgotten.

Certain other, quieter, games were also played, of chance or fortune-telling. Ramses is often depicted playing draughts on the threshold of his palace in the company of one of his favourite concubines. They also played "odds and evens" with dice, this being a symbolic representation of the four elements: earth, air, fire and water.

Sometimes bones or shells were used. The simple pleasures of *kollabismos* were enjoyed, as in

Greece: kneeling on the ground with his eyes blindfolded, a player had to guess the identity of the player who had struck him... on the bottom!

Another game consisted in endeavouring to snatch from each other a small hoop, by means of hooked rods, probably of metal; and the success of a player seems to have depended on extricating his own from the adversary's rod, and then snatching up the hoop before he had time to stop it.

One of the more ancient games played by the Egyptians was the game of the serpent. It was played on a low table on which a picture of a coiled snake had been painted or inlaid, with its head innermost. The body was divided into various proportions. Each player had a number of pawns: three lions, three lionnesses, white balls,

red balls. Some of these pieces are genuine works of art. The rules of the games were a compromise between the game of the goose and draughts.

The draughts board itself was divided either into thirty or thirty-two squares. When play was over, both board and pieces were carefully placed back in special cases made of ebony or other precious woods.

Juggling was sometimes performed by amateurs. Egyptians, both young and old, were experts with a ball, women perhaps particularly so. In some games the ball was simply thrown back and forth, while the game could be made much more difficult when the player was required to jump before catching the ball, to keep one hand on his head, one foot in the air or one knee bent. In some games several balls were kept going at the same time,

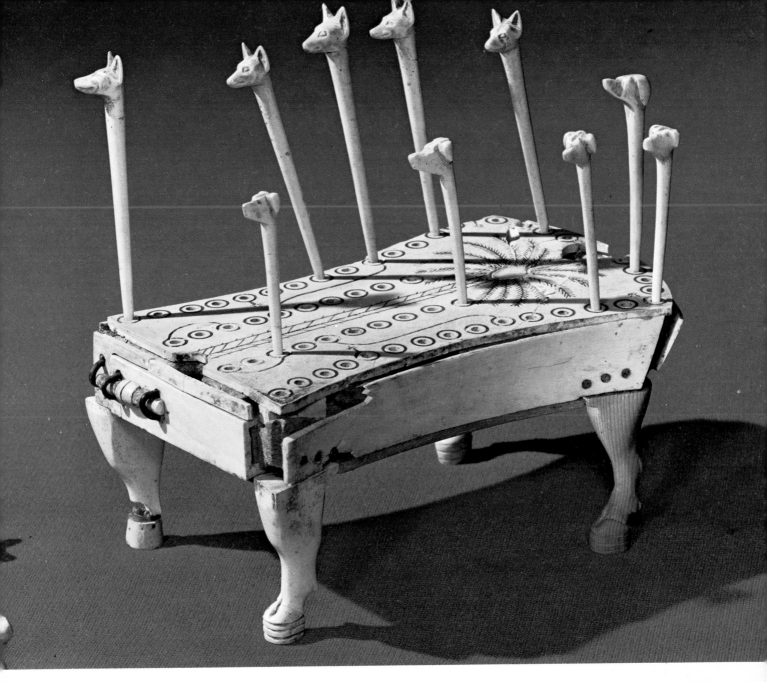

Upper left, table for the
"game of the serpent".

Below, two dancing girls
next to a buffet.
Above, this very curious
instrument enabled one to
play the game of "the dog
and the jackal".
Right, four young girls
playing ball.

being thrown unexpectedly to several players at a time.

Losers had to make a forfeit, sometimes serving as a horse for the winner and carrying him, in triumph, around either side-saddle or astride the back of the hapless loser.

Another game consisted in throwing a knife, or pointed weapon, into a block of wood, in which each player was required to strike his adversary's, or more probably to fix his own in the centre of a ring painted on the wood; and his success depended on being able to ring his weapon most frequently, or get closest to the centre.

In another popular game of chance, each player had a little ball and three scoops, the idea being to move the ball around keeping it under one or the other of the scoops, so that the other players could not see it. It required great sleight of hand.

Another way the evening might end was drinking pure and simple; the guest would slump on their cushions and wait for the servants to come and fill up their glasses—which they proceeded to do, endlessly and copiously. Guests of both sexes would get quite helplessly drunk, eventually being reduced to vomiting all over the floor, collapsing by their chairs and then having to be taken home half-conscious and inert.

GAMES OF SKILL OR COMPETITION

Egyptians were, however, very concerned with the beauty of their bodies. This is why, in circumstances other than the dinner-parties which we have just described, they engaged in games which were vastly better for the health.

They were particularly fond of weight-lifting, which they used to practise with bags full of sand. They also had tests of strength; in one of these, two men sat back to back, their elbows interlocked and tried to stand up while tipping each other off balance. Or they would catch each other's hands and spin around until one of the players became too dizzy to go on.

Wrestling and mock combat of all sorts were also popular. Players fought naked, with only a leather belt, having rubbed their bodies with oil to make them slippery; they approached each other with arms outstretched, knees bent, seeking to immobilize each other.

Anything went, as the saying goes: it was permissible to seize one's opponent's head or neck, to try to strangle him, trip him or grab him bodily. Even if one of the fighters fell to the ground the fight went on; the loser could get badly hurt.

In order for this game to end, the loser had to recognize his defeat by making a conventional sign—often a special word—in which case the winner would let go.

Other types of fight involved the use of a cane. The hands were protected by a sort of shield made of a wooden plate and a piece of wicker-work covering all the knuckles. It was a very violent game.

Instead of a cane, the players sometimes used a *neboot,* or large stick held in both hands. This exercise was very popular, as can be seen from the paintings. Despite the fact that it was preceded by a highly civilized ritual, it could be extremely violent, as if the players were really in earnest. The wounded had to be picked up off the battle-field, and the maimed limped away from the scene of their defeat painfully.

A refined form of this game took place on a barge; losers then fell into the water, where they were regarded as most definitely beaten, once and for all.

The "game of the kid" was a sort of obstacle race, in which the obstacle consisted of the interwoven bodies of two players who tried to grab in mid-air the person who was supposed to jump over them. The runner had to announce that he was starting, and run as fast as he could, but he was sometimes caught in mid-air and would crash painfully to the ground.

Track racing, including handicap races, was very popular. In the case of children, the handicap consisted in starting last, if one was older, or running on one's knees, with one's hands tied or on all fours.

Dancing was the favourite game for girls. They used a mirror or a stick to make their arm movements more elegant, they attached a weight or a ball to their hair in order to mark the rhythm more clearly, and they would turn, leap and balance endlessly. There were solo and group dances. Girls used to accompany themselves by singing the praises of Hathor, patron of all pleasures.

Bull-fights were also popular. Men would prove their valour by hurling themselves at the bulls

with their bare hands; they would try to catch them or turn them over, while avoiding being gored by means of quick manoeuvres. These fights took place on the *dromos*, the avenue which lead to the entrance to the temple in each major town. Strabo describes one which was held at Memphis, outside the temple of Vulcan. Others are shown in the earliest paintings at Thebes or the caves of Beni-Hassan.

Slaves do not seem to have been involved in these games; nor do they seem to have been pitted in combat against savage beasts for the amusement of a cold-blooded audience.

As a result of all these exercises, the bodies of the Egyptians of the Pharaonic period were beautifully sculpted; they knew that physical beauty depended on the right kind of training.

THE EGYPTIAN SENSE OF HUMOUR

The Egyptians were a gay people, with a lively sense of humour. They also excelled in the art of caricature. There are many humorous scenes in the paintings: for example, a group of people at a party have manifestly lost their balance as a result of drink, and are shown in grotesque poses by the artist.

Other comical scenes from the paintings include people falling, cakes falling over a boat-load of mourners, practical jokes, etc. For example, a monkey which had been trained to hold the oil-lamps during a party is shown tipping their contents over the glittering but inebriated assembly.

Even the mighty did not escape from this penchant for caricature: for example, there are countless statues of Akhenaton which show the monarch with a goatlike profile and a fat belly which do nothing for the dignity of his office. Portrait artists seemed to latch onto peculiar traits. "Bubbles" are seen attached to the mouths of people in a group that is enjoying a good joke.

Numerous stories were told about life in the harem; a great deal of intrigue seems to have gone on, not to mention the abundance of saucy remarks and suggestive innuendo which accompanied such stories.

Despite the solemn appearance of the ancient Egyptians in the monumental record of their lives, they do seem to have been capable of a good laugh from time to time, to say the least.

6. MORE ENTERTAINMENTS AND PASTIMES

HUNTING

From the very rich to the very poor, the noble to the fellah, Egyptians loved hunting. Their country, of course, was particularly well stocked with game; hunting was more than a sport, as it provided the population with a substantial source of nourishment.

Apart from that, the destruction of animals harmful to harvest or livestock was an obligation. It also happened that offerings of game were thought to be particularly well received by the gods.

Egyptians thus indulged without a moment's remorse in this pleasant and at the same time profitable pastime which is described in detail in the mural paintings.

Hunting could take various forms; it could be done by single individuals or groups, with weapons ranging from the bow and arrow to the club and boomerang, on foot or on horseback with a pack of dogs. Game could also be tracked down in a flat boat made of pleated reeds, which could slip silently through the thickets on the marshes where the water birds lived.

Hunting in the desert was perhaps the most spectacular form of the chase, and as such was reserved for the nobles and the very rich. But it was also a source of profit for the other members of the party. The lords would wait on horseback while their helpers used nets to encircle a large, judiciously chosen area. All concerned were admirably well acquainted with the habits of the game they were pursuing. They used to notice particularly the watering holes where the animals would go to drink in the cool hours of the day. This might be a large pool which had not dried up after the end of the flood, or a branch of a river reaching into the desert. The most favourable terrain was chosen: a dead end of some sort, perhaps the end of a valley hemmed in by steep rocky walls, a kind of natural arena from which there was no escape.

They knew, of course, that cornered animals would not even try to rush at the cliffs surrounding them, and would choose to stay put.

The chosen piece of land was thus closed off by two nets. The one at the end was absolutely tight; that placed at the entrance was solidly kept in position by stakes embedded in the ground, so as to let in the hunters, who were waiting calmly behind a boulder or some bushes.

Wisely chosen bait could also be used to attract the game, which would gradually move into the trap in large numbers—after which the second net would fall.

The slaughter then began. The lords, on horseback, spear in hand, would drive the game deeper into the trap, and then, placed in strategic positions, they would kill vast numbers of them.

Arrows came raining down. Their tips were usually metal but could also be of stone. In keeping with an ancient technique the string was drawn back as far as the chest, while the bow itself was not raised to the level of the ear; apparently this gave added power.

The fellahs and farmers used a very effective kind of slingshot. The throwing club was also commonly used: it was about 15 to 18 inches wide and had a slightly curved tip. Since it had a very good aerodynamic shape and was made of very heavy wood, it could be thrown, by someone with a little training, over quite long distances.

The boomerang was also used, though it was usually reserved for the lords. This weapon was considered more of a sport than a method of hunting, because its effectiveness in the field was not adequate.

Left, hunting for birds and, below, for game.

A wide range of game was thus tracked and slain in this way: the wild goat, or ibex, a real delicacy, the silk-skinned gazelle—which made such an elegant upholstery—the oryx, an antelope with slender, tapering horns, known for that reason as the "sabre antelope", the wild buffalo, which was so fond of wading up to his neck in the muddy waters of the Nile, the deer, the *kebsh*, or wild sheep, the succulent hare and the porcupine. All these animals would end up on the table of gourmets, having first been cooked by the finest chefs available.

Besides these, however, they hunted the hyena, the jackal, fox and the *fennec*, all of which were fearsome predators, dreaded by the farmers, who had only too often seen poultry, lambs and eggs disappear between their fangs. Crocodiles were considered a nuisance only in Upper Egypt.

Wolves and, above all, leopards were slaughtered for the beauty of their fur. The ostrich was highly prized on account of its feathers, which were put to elegant use in interior decorating and in making the fans of society ladies.

There were large numbers of highly esteemed game birds; for example, the plump geese of the Nile, whose flesh was such a welcome food for the lower classes, and ducks, snipe, cranes, teal, scoter and other water-fowl. As for the partridge, bustard or quail, they were abundant along the slopes where the vineyards were situated.

Egyptians did not always kill game birds. Sometimes they would take them live in fine-meshed nets; then, displaying great knowledge of bird-breeding, they would take them home and raise them or domesticate them. They used a wide range of traps. One consisted of a net stretched over a wooden frame, with two hinged semi-circular flaps attached to a central rod. The trap was kept open by strings, papyrus or cat gut. As soon as the bait, in the middle, was touched, the net would fall.

Another trap was square, and built around a central frame. The Egyptians were very clever at building traps of this sort. One thinks, for instance, of the huge apparatus installed in the treasury of Rhampsinitus. A thief got caught in it, and the spring held him so tight that even his brother's attempts to free him were in vain.

Fowl thus trapped were taken in cubic cages to the farms. They were fed and fattened until the time came for them to be eaten. When the number of cages was inadequate, the birds were immobilized by having their feet, beaks and necks tied together.

Some furry game-animals were also taken alive and then domesticated and trained for the hunt back at the farm.

Dogs were the preferred animal for this purpose. There were watch-dogs, usually long-legged greyhounds—a dwarf strain known as *ketket* was particularly highly thought of. Sheep dogs were somewhat cruder but still very well trained. But hunting dogs were even more useful; they used to be raised in whole packs at a time.

Farmers trained cats as retrievers, and to good effect. Realizing that they were terrified of water, their masters never sent these animals after water-fowl, however.

They also used decoys—geese, ducks or other species whose females, deeply attached to their nests, would never leave it, and would, instead, attract other birds. They also used the civet-cat, to beat the game from the bush and frighten them. All of these aids were highly useful in the hunt.

Hunting parties were often occasions for splendid merrymaking. The lord would invite his whole family, his friends and take along all his servants. The party would set out on horseback, in chariots or, sometimes, on boats. In the latter, they would move forward through the reeds or other aquatic plants, across the lakes formed by the Nile flood, the tributaries of the Nile and the canals.

While the hunt was on everyone had a good time, with picnics and general fun and games.

Hunting was always rewarded by an ample bag.

FISHING

The Nile was crammed with fish. It is a gentle river which yields readily to the passage of all sorts of boats, from skiffs to barges. Since Egypt had only a slender strip of fertile soil and very little grazing land, meat was a rarity.

Curiously enough, however, fish was taboo. This might seem even a contradictory fact, for a country which was effectively huddled around its river. But it was definitely considered impure. For example, the hieroglyph for "abomination" is represented by a fish.

Yet the pictorial record of daily life in ancient Egypt is full of fishing scenes, even of miraculous catches, while in the temples the votive table was often depicted as being fully laden with fish.

Perhaps on account of the predominance of material need over abstract ideology, the meatless peasantry found that fish was a great delicacy. For the fellah, it was a second gift of the Nile—and may Osiris, who died with each dry season, only to be reborn with the flood, be praised for it.

Everybody, young or old, dignitary or peasant, loved to go fishing; the methods used, however, varied according to one's physical condition and one's tastes.

One could indulge in the tranquil pleasures of angling, sitting alone, on the banks of a canal or lake; the fisherman would sometimes take along his chair or folding seat, even a mattress, on which he could stretch out in comfort.

Anglers went after the big fish; when one had bitten, it would be clubbed to death or speared with a harpoon or bident.

Most people used a light papyrus boat or some other kind of light craft in order to find their fish under the reeds. They would lay their bait during the evening, and then come back the next morning, confident of a good catch. They would use a landing-net to bring ashore the heavier fish. Strings were stretched out across the boat, and

the fish were hung up by the gills.

This kind of fishing was for fun. But the peasant, who was more concerned with efficiency and profit, used nets and pots. In shallow marshes he would lay down a broad pot in the shape of a bottle, or a double pot, with two compartments. It was half-covered with reeds. The fish attracted by the bait then swam in unsuspectingly, but were then unable to get back out, as the grass and the mesh of the net prevented them. Some particularly well-stocked parts of the river were popular fishing places with the local people.

On a larger scale, several people could join forces and use a seine-net. A dozen men, two boats and a broad and very heavy rectangular net were needed for this purpose. A full-scale expedition had to be mounted on such occasions. The net was weighted with stones, so that it fell to the bottom of the lake. Raising the net was a tricky business, involving accurate timing. It had to be done quickly, as some fish might get away; indeed, the larger fish had sometimes to be killed with a harpoon or mallet. The harpoons consisted of a wooden handle and a heavy metal hook.

Not content with the abundance of the waters of the river, its tributaries and the lakes, the Egyptians used to build large ponds on their properties, rather like the *vivaria* of the Romans. They stocked these with the fish they caught and then proceeded to fatten them.

Fishing therefore had a dual advantage for Egyptians: pleasure and nourishment.

The richness of the fertile lands was matched by that of the waters of the Nile, as can be seen from the various fishing scenes shown on these two pages. Bottom, a scene of mourning.

CELEBRATIONS

The day-to-day life of the Egyptians was broken by large numbers of festivities, all of them of religious origin. At least once a year, and in each temple, the local god was brought out in great pomp, to return the visits which the villagers had made to his temple all year long. On this occasion, processions were held behind the effigies of the god which were carried along the streets of the town. An enormous celebration was held on this day.

On holidays such as these, the peasants were not required to work, the rich offered banquets and drink to the poor, and the servants themselves participated in the merrymaking. The priests encouraged the festivities, and indeed organized the entertainment themselves, feeling that it could not fail to bolster their own authority and prestige.

Being by nature gay and fond of good living, the Egyptians took the maximum advantage of any opportunity for a good time. Some festivals attracted the population of a whole region, as in the case of the coming-out of Bastit at Bast. Herodotus attended some of these ceremonies, and describes them for us in detail.

He mentions the large number of boats which converged on the site of the celebrations, loaded down with men and women, laughing and singing, to the accompaniment of flutes and castanets. The atmosphere was joyous, as the happy sounds of revelry and banter echoed from one boat to another, all across the river, in the midst of dancing, excitement... and drink.

According to Herodotus, the seven hundred thousand pilgrims who visited Bast drank as much wine in that one week as the whole of Egypt throughout the rest of the year. An exaggeration, perhaps, but a clue to the atmosphere on these occasions.

An important ceremony was that of the reliquaries, or shrines, which is mentioned on the Rosetta Stone and is often depicted in the temple paintings. The reliquaries were carried on long wooden shafts, resting on the shoulders of the priests; they were carried throughout the town and the region, before being placed on a plinth at the entrance to the temple. The population would recite long litanies in honour of the god, and hymns would be sung. Offering were made. The participants were full of fervour, but also full of joy.

The triumph of the kings was also a very solemn feast, at which popular gaiety and enthusiasm could be given free rein. Crowns and bouquets of flowers were offered to the dignitaries. The populace applauded and chanted expressions of thanks.

Among the anniversaries, the most remarkable was that of Niloa, or the evocation of the benefits of the Nile flood, which was offered in honour of Amon. The ceremonies were held at Opet during the second or the third month of the flood, and the entire population took part. The farmers were relieved from all work in any case, as their lands were covered in water; boats could move about easily on the swollen waters. A vast crowd congregated at the temple of Opet.

Merchants selling food, flowers and fabrics stood ready, waiting to wander through the crowd. The priests had prepared the portable boats of the Theban family which were to be carried shoulder-

high during the ceremonies. The most imposing of these was that of Amon, adorned with rams heads, while that of Mut had two female heads with vultures' beaks; the boat of Khonsou was dominated by falcons' heads.

The model boats passed between the two rows of sphinxes and were carried to the river, where huge and lavishly decorated vessels were waiting to take them on board. They were so heavy that they had to be hauled along by an army of men, while the spectators shouted encouragingly. When they reached the Nile they floated along between the massed ranks of the populace on either side; mobile restaurants were set up wherever the need arose, dancers, both male and female, performed, and, of course, everyone drank.

The votive boat of Amon was brought out one second time during the year, for the festival of the valley. It crossed the river at Luksor to visit the Pharaoh in the hypostyle hall at Ramesseum; this time the festivities lasted ten days.

Abydos was a well-known place of pilgrimage in honour of Osiris, whose head is thought to have been buried there. Just as the vegetation of the Nile valley was beginning to re-appear under the influence of the flood, Osiris was reborn to the acclamation of the people.

All these festivities had the role of an invocation: if the rites were not adhered to, the wrath of the gods was to be feared.

In honour of certain divinities games and gymnastic competitions were held. At Chemmis, Perseus was honoured in this way. The combattants were rewarded with gifts of cattle, hides or clothes.

The priests drew on every resource of the imagination in order to enhance the spectacle of the coming-out of the gods. They organized a grand theatrical performance relating the life of the god. Great attention was paid to costumes and decor, so that these mysteries took place in an atmosphere of euphoria. The spectators were of course well acquainted with the life of the god, but never tired of seeing its principal episodes repeated for their edification. They even took part themselves by lamenting loudly at certain dramatic moments, clapping their hands and crying out for joy at the moments of triumph.

At the end of the performance, they continued to be excited for many hours, during which they stayed in the same place and danced endlessly.

These popular dramas were played outside the temple, in the courtyard or between the pylons; they were certainly the principal attraction of the festivities.

Strabo mentions one of these, "during which a dense crowd of people hurried down the canal from Alexandria to Canopus to join the festive meeting. Day and night it was covered with boats bringing men and women, singing and dancing with the greatest licentiousness; and at Canopus

itself inns were opened upon the canal purposely for the convenience of indulging in these amusements."

MUSIC

The Egyptians loved music. Pythagoras, who was so impressed by their wisdom, noted that they paid particular attention to the study of music; Plato, who was also an attentive observer of the social scene along the banks of the Nile, states that they thought it was beneficial for youth.

However, there was music and music, it seems. Strabo confirms that, besides letters, Egyptian children also learned music and singing, all under strict State authorization and supervision. It was felt that an excess of music, particularly of the sort meant for entertainment alone, was harmful, and could lead to dissolute and effeminate behaviour. The main objection against over-exposure to music was that it tended to excite the mind to an extent difficult to control. Worse still, according to Diodorus, it was a waste of time.

Yet Egyptians believed that music was of divine origin; the number of pictures of musicians in the sculptures and bas-reliefs, as well as the paintings, is clear evidence of the importance attached to music. Athenaeus tells us that the Greeks and the barbarians learned their music from Egyptian refugees.

Among the Egyptians, the Alexandrians were most renowned for their musical art. There were professionals who used to take part in private or public shows, and who travelled in troupes around the different towns looking for work. It was frequently slaves, or persons of lowly rank, and never the members of noble families who performed in this way. The nobles did learn music; however, they remained amateurs.

The number of known instruments shows that music was not a rudimentary art. There were numerous types of flute and oboe. The double flute was made of two reeds placed at an acute angle. The harps were very bulky, with numerous strings. We know that they had some harps of monumental size, with huge resonant chambers, and others which were much smaller, and portable.

Right, two flutes and a lute.

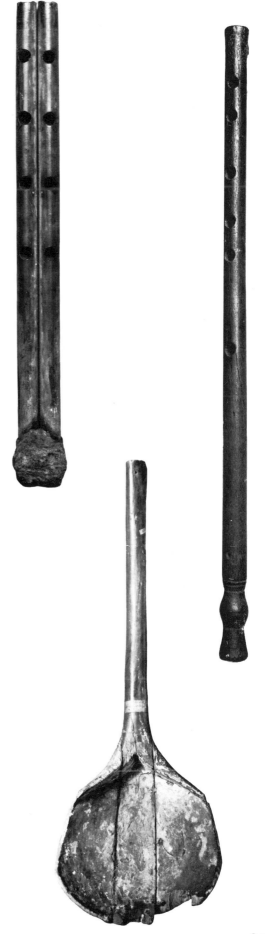

DANCING

In all civilisations, dancing has always accompanied music. It might be very ritualistic, though in some cases it sought to vary the figures to the greatest extent possible. During the religious ceremonies the classical steps and the conventional attitudes were respected, but at private parties or at the kind of festivities which started spontaneously after the ceremonies, much improvisation went on.

One could dance either singly or in groups, with the sexes either together or apart. The men danced with immense vigour, accompanying their motions with rhythmic jumps. The women used slower rhythms, these being better able to display the elegance and the grace of their movements and the supple beauty of their bodies. For either style

They were beautifully decorated, and were enriched with a sculpted head. The cithara also came in two versions, a portable one with five strings, and a bigger one, with ten.

The lute was commonly used; it was a small elongated box with holes; the strings were secured to its wooden neck.

There were many percussion instruments: they included the tambourine, round or square, small or large, and the castanets, consisting of two ivory plates hung from a necklace. These instruments were used mainly during festivities and religious processions, in which they kept the beat for the marchers.

A relief painted on a wall of a tomb at Sakkarah shows singers and flautists in a crouching position. The conductor is raising his hand to indicate the beat; the singers are accompanying themselves by clapping their hands.

Singing was a very popular activity: the songs were often improvisations in honour of the hosts and their guests, and, especially, hymns in honour of the gods.

The superb dish shown opposite shows a young female musician seated on a cushion.

86

Above and below, highly expressive dance motions.

of dancing, strict training was essential.

As we see in a scene painted about 1,300 years before Socrates, the women performed pirouettes forwards and backwards, cartwheels, the splits and backward flips. Sometimes they performed these exercises in pairs, one of the female dancers standing up and the other on her back, with her head between the legs of the first girl. They would do pirouettes in that position, head up and head down alternately. These were difficult exercises, acrobatics in fact, which could only be done by professionals.

The dances were sometimes lascivious and the garb of the dancing girls, such as it was, was highly suggestive, by means of the transparency of the fabric and the motion of the veils. The modern observer could well feel he was watching a modern "girlie" show: on a bas-relief painted at Sakkarah, the members of the dancing troupe are shown wearing an extremely small loincloth; they are lifting their legs in time, and their hair is tied up in a pony tail to which they have attached a heavy metal disk, the swinging motions of which emphasize the rhythm of their dance steps.

The professional dancers were slaves or persons

Right, an acrobatic dancing girl.

of lower rank, just like the musicians. In any self-respecting household there were a certain number of serving girls capable of performing for the amusement of their masters, besides the real artists and professionals.

Yet the girls and young women of Egyptian high society were all good dancers. This activity was for them, as we have seen, a favourite and regular game.

By dancing, all of them were in fact worshipping Hathor, the goddess of love, happiness, dancing and music. Like all the Egyptian gods, Hathor, before the advent of anthropomorphism, was depicted as an animal—in this case, a cow. She later acquired a human head and body, but she kept the two horns which are always seen on images of her, and are her distinctive emblem.

89

7. THE PEASANTS AND AGRICULTURE

THE FLOOD

One cannot talk of Egyptian agriculture without mentioning the Nile. Without the Nile there would be no Egypt and no crops of any sort. As Herodotus put it in a pithy expression: "Egypt is a gift of the Nile". The river is so crucial in the everyday life of the country that the first calendar, drawn up even before the First Dynasty, is based on it. The year was divided into three seasons: the Flood, or inundation, from June to September, Emergence, from October to February, and Drought, during the four last months. Since agriculture proceeded at the pace of the Nile, the social life did likewise.

A whole year, with all its hopes and misfortunes, abundance or famine, depended on the river overflowing its banks to the right degree. The officials in charge of the Nilometers began to examine the changes in the level of the waters in these specially gradated wells at the Cataracts, about the end of May, or the beginning of June; and a change from the previous clearness of the stream was soon observed in its red and turbid state, caused by the rains from the mountains of Abyssinia. It then assumed a green appearance; and during this period its water being deemed unwholesome, a supply previously laid up in jars was used until it had re-assumed its turbid but wholesome red colour.

This explains the remark of Aristides, that "the Egyptians are the only people who preserve water in jars, and calculate its age as other nations do that of wine;" and the reason for adopting water jars as emblems of the inundation may probably be derived from this custom of laying up the pure water of the Nile in jars, about the season, or at the first approach, of the inundation; though the calculation of the age of the water must be considered a Greek exaggeration.

It was perhaps this change in the appearance of the river which led the Egyptians to represent the god Nilus both of a red and a blue colour,—indicating the river during the turbid state of the inundation, and the clearness of the low Nile.

In the beginning of August the canals were again opened, and the waters once more overflowed the plain. That part nearest the desert, being the lowest level, was first inundated; as the bank itself, being the highest, was the last part submerged, except in the Delta, where the levels were more uniform, and where, during the high inundations, the whole land, with the exception of its isolated villages, was under water.

As the Nile rose, the peasants were careful to remove the flocks and herds from the lowlands; and when a sudden irruption of the water, owing to the bursting of a dyke or an unexpected and unusual increase of the river, overflowed the fields and pastures, they were seen hurrying to the spot, on foot or in boats, to rescue the animals, and to remove them to the high ground above the reach of the inundation.

Guards were placed to watch the dykes which protected the lowlands, and the utmost care was taken to prevent any sudden influx of water, which might endanger the produce still growing there, the cattle, or the villages. And of such importance was the preservation of the dykes, that a strong guard of cavalry and infantry was always in attendance for their protection; certain officers of responsibility were appointed to superintend them; large sums of money ware annually expended for their maintenance and repairs; and in the time of the Romans, any person found destroying a dyke was condemned to hard labour in the public works or in the mines, or to be branded and transported to the Oasis.

According to Strabo, the system was so admirably managed, "that art contrived sometimes to supply what nature denied, and, by means of canals and embankments, there was little difference in the quantity of land irrigated, whether the flood was deficient or abundant."

In some parts of Egypt the villages were frequently liable to be flooded, when the Nile rose to a more than ordinary height, endangering the lives and property of the inhabitants; and when their crude brick houses had been long exposed to the damp, the foundations gave way, and the fallen walls, saturated with water, were once more mixed with the mud from which they had been extracted. On these occasions the blessings of the Nile inflicted heavy losses on the inhabitants; and, as Pliny observes, "if the rise of the water exceeded sixteen cubits, a famine was the result, as when it only reached the height of twelve." In another place he says, "A proper inundation is of sixteen cubits; ... in twelve cubits the country suffers from famine, and feels a deficiency even in thirteen;

fourteen cause joy, fifteen security, sixteen delight; at seventeen, panic."

One readily understands, therefore, the great anxiety with which the rise of the Nile was followed each year, on account of the immense potential benefit or harm which it could cause to a country which depended so entirely on it.

During the inundation, when the Nile had been admitted by the canals into the interior, and the fields were subjected to the fertilising influence of its waters, the peasantry indulged in various amusements which this leisure period gave them time to enjoy. Their cattle were housed, and supplied with dry food, which had been previously prepared for the purpose; the tillage of the land and all agricultural occupations were suspended; and this season was celebrated as a harvest home, with games and recreations of every kind. They indulged in feasting and the luxuries of the table; games were organized and prizes of cattle were awarded to the winners. Wrestling, gymnastics and bull-fights helped keep the peasants entertained, and spared them the pernicious effects of an excessive period of idleness.

The Pharaoh had another—and less entertaining—method for keeping his subjects busy: he needed extra hands for his various construction projects. Curiously, the people did not seem to mind contributing their labour to such enterprises, and temples and pyramids were thus built in the midst of popular enthusiasm.

When the waters receded, the appearance of the land had changed; much litigation then ensued about the precise boundaries of various pieces of property. Fields were not enclosed, and the markers had been usually swept away by the waters; the banks of the river had perhaps collapsed and some land may have been lost. It therefore became necessary to determine where each property began and ended, *inter alia,* for the orderly collection of State taxes. A corps of cord-stretchers, the ancestors of our modern surveyors, worked on such problems. In this way, through material necessity, the Egyptians invented geometry.

DOWN ON THE FARM

The bas-reliefs contain numerous scenes depicting the fellahs at work. A prime task of theirs, as we have seen, was that of saving from the waters

everything which could be taken to safety; they also had to protect houses and barns by means of light dykes. They also had to extend the benefits of the Nile to those lands which were too far from the river to be directly flooded by it. For this they used many methods, but principally the digging of channels. There were many of these which reached all the way to the sands of the desert. It was possible to supply these channels with water using a rudimentary but highly efficient device known as the *shadoof*. A long pole was balanced over the well, with a scoop at one end and a counter-weight at the other. The fellah had to pull the string to lower the bucket into the well; once it was full, however, it came back up on its own, and a slight shove was all that was required to tip its contents into the channel.

Waterwheels equipped with a continuous row of scoops were also used. When all else failed, they simply got into a boat and brought back from the river a number of buckets filled with water, which they then carried to the fields.

As the Nile subsided, the water was retained in the fields by proper embankments; and the mouths of the canals being again closed, it was prevented from returning into the falling stream. By this means the irrigation of the land was prolonged considerably, and fertilising effects of the inundation continued, until the water was absorbed. They did not end until November, when the mud was dried up completely by the blazing rays of the Egyptian sun.

"In no country, says Herodotus, do they gather their seed with so little labour. They are not obliged to trace deep furrows with the plough, to break the clods, nor to partition out their fields into numerous forms, as other people do; but when the river of itself overflows the land, and the water retires again, they sow their fields, driving the pigs over them to tread in the seed; and this being done, every one patiently awaits the harvest."

There was no doubt about it—Egypt really was a gift of the Nile!

LAND TENURE

Officials known as *nomarchs* superintended all the agricultural regulations established for the interests of the peasant, or connected with the

Facing, servants storing corn in a granary, in the presence of a superintendent and a scribe.

claims of Government. It seems unlikely that the Government interfered directly with the peasant respecting the nature of the produce he cultivated, or that any of the vexations of later times existed under the Pharaohs. The peasants were naturally supposed to have obtained, from actual observation, the most accurate knowledge on all subjects connected with husbandry; and, as Diodorus observes, "being from their infancy brought up to agricultural pursuits, they far excelled the husbandmen of other countries, and had become acquainted with the capabilities of the land, the mode of irrigation, the exact season for sowing and reaping, as well as all the most useful secrets connected with the harvest, which they had derived from their ancestors, and had improved by their own experience."

"They rent," says the same historian, "the arable land belonging to the kings, the priests, and the military class, for a small sum, and employ their

A rich landowner checking his cattle, which are being led by fellahs.
Right, person carrying poultry; the harvest and the storage of grain.

whole time in the tillage of their farms;" and the labourers who cultivated land for the rich peasant or other landed proprietors were superintended by the steward or owner of the estate, who had authority over them, and the power of condemning delinquents to be beaten; the paintings of the tombs frequently represent a person of consequence inspecting the tillage of the field, either seated in a chariot, walking, or leaning on his staff, accompanied by a favourite dog.

The condition of the husbandmen, however, is not described in glowing terms by the scribe Pentaur in the Sallier Papyrus I. When he would gather in the crops, it says, the caterpillar ravaged the kitchen garden, and the beasts, or hippopotami, ate up the other things; rats invaded the fields, birds landed on the crops, beasts consumed and sparrows stole what the farmer had planted with such immense effort. The ploughshare rusted, beasts and horses died while ploughing; the tax-collector took the farmer's sheaves, while police and slaves added to the squabbling: and if the husbandman drank, his wife and children suffered for it.

THE PASTORAL LIFE

The rich landowners possessed a large stock of sheep, goats, and cattle; gazelles, and other wild animals of the desert, were tamed and reared with great care on their estates; and they gave the greatest attention to the breeding of horses, asses, and other beasts of burden. The pastors, it is true, were a class apart from the peasantry, and one which was held in disrepute by the Egyptians, partly in consequence of the nature of their occupation, and partly from the feeling excited against them by the remembrance of cruelties exercised upon their countrymen by a tribe of shepherds in the distant past. Swineherds were viewed with distaste, but this ostracism applied only to those who actually looked after the flocks, and not to the breeders and farmers.

The status of the former was so lowly that they lived in makeshift shelters made of reeds, and easily transportable. Very often they were shepherds by heredity, father and son replacing each other successively over the generations. Their

The donkey was an important part of the peasant's life. He was the closest servant and helpmate of man. Above, a scene in the butcher's shop.

life was not monotonous, as they had to keep a watch on the fluctuations of the Nile and make sure the animals were moved to the right place at the right time. They were experts when it came to choosing the right piece of land for their animals, avoiding marshy areas where the younger animals might drown, and steering their charges well clear of voracious crocodiles. They branded their livestock so as to prevent theft.

They were exceedingly diligent, not just because liked their work, but also because they were accountable to the superintendent. This latter official actually decided when the animals should be moved out, what kind of treatment should be given in case of epidemic or disease; but the herdsman himself risked a beating if he should fail in his responsibilities, and was held accountable for accidents. theft. even incorrect births.

Of course, the number of head of livestock was checked periodically, together with their state of health, anticipated births, etc., and all in writing.

BUREAUCRACY ON THE FARM

Everything in Egypt was done by writing. Scribes were employed on all occasions, whether to settle public or private questions, and no bargain of any consequence was made without being sanctioned by the authority of a written document.

Such pervasive bureaucracy also extended, as one might expect, to the farm: the cattle were brought into a yard attached to the steward's house, or into the farmyard, and counted by the superintendent in the presence of the scribes. Every care was taken to prevent or detect frauds, and the stick was freely administered, whenever the peasant or the shepherd neglected the animals entrusted to his care.

Scribes were thus important, if not indispensable, figures on the farm—as elsewhere in Egyptian society!

Two antelopes, a bull and more donkeys. The skinny peasant shown left, leaning on his stick, is a cattle-driver.

The tools and instruments of the countryside: hoe, whip and, right, a pick.

THE TOOLS OF THE EGYPTIAN PEASANT

On some occasions they used the plough, but were contented, as Diodorus and Columella observe, with "tracing slight furrows with light ploughs on the surface of the land; and others followed the plough with wooden hoes to break the clods of the rich and tenacious soil."

It consisted of a share, two handles, and the pole or beam; which last was inserted into the lower end of the stilt, or the base of the handles, and was strengthened by a rope connecting it with the heel. It had no coulter, nor were wheels applied to any Egyptian plough: but it is probable that the point was shod with a metal sock, either of bronze or iron. It was drawn by two oxen; and the ploughman guided and drove them with a long goad, without using reins. He was sometimes accompanied by an assistant armed with a whip.

The mode of yoking the beasts was exceedingly simple. Across the extremity of the pole, a wooden yoke or cross bar, about fifty-five inches or five feet in length, was fastened by a strap, lashed backwards and forwards over a prominence, projecting from the centre of the yoke, which corresponded to a similar peg, or knob, at the end of the pole. At either end of the yoke was a flat or slightly concave projection, of semicircular form, which rested on a pad placed upon the withers of the animal.

Sometimes the draught, instead of being from the shoulder, was from the head, the yoke being tied to the base of the horns; and in religious ceremonies oxen frequently drew the bier, or the sacred shrine, by a rope fastened to the upper part of the horns, without either yoke or pole.

Two persons were needed to drive the plough; the one who held the handles had to be stronger, because his work was much harder. He had to weigh down upon the plough and move every muscle in his body, while the other person could be a child or a woman since the work involved, while important, was not tiring, consisting, as it did, of guiding the animals pulling the plough. Sometimes he would carry a whip, though he could

also do this job by me[...]

In a classical scene, [...] in the soil, while ano[...] wooden handle and a m[...] is chopping down trees a[...] species, tamarisk, syca[...] that provided timber [...] agricultural equipment, a[...]

The Egyptians had n[...] since these tools were no[...]

Left, bottom, a beekeeper.

Slaughter-house scene and harvest.
Above, the scribes are noting, carefully write down the amount of the crop.

BUSINESS

Commerce was based on gold, silver and copper, the prices always being set in terms of weight. Until the introduction of coins bearing the authoritative State seal, the weight system had been the only way of preserving the honesty and the interests of all concerned. Gold is seen in circulation on the paintings from the tombs starting in the reign of Thoutmes III, a great conqueror, who had followed his mother-in-law, the famous Hatshepsout, the woman-Pharaoh.

The paintings of Thebes frequently represent persons in the act of weighing gold, or the purchase of articles in the market. This continued to be the custom when rings of gold and silver were used in Egypt for money, and even to the time of the Ptolemies, who established a coinage of gold, silver and copper in the country.

A scribe or notary marked down the amount of the weight, whatever the commodity might be: and this document, being given to the parties, completely sanctioned the bargain, and served as a pledge that justice had been done to them.

An unexpected helpmate for man: the monkey! This one, shown above, is indulging a fondness for figs.
Right, a flock of ducks.

soil. The pick-axe was extremely rudimentary, consisting of a handle. a cross-piece and a wooden blade. It used to break often. The shovel was nothing more than a simple hoe. The scythe was used for two purposes, harvesting and also cutting the fodder of the livestock or the straw used for making matting. It was short and broad.

The sower used to carry the seeds in a small basket hanging from his neck or his left arm on a piece of leather thonging. He tossed the seed with his right hand, in the manner known as "broadcast" and it simply fell on the ploughed soil.

In this way, and often in the mud. crops such as wheat, barley, clover and flax were sown. The harvest took place in the spring. This method of cultivation was known as *shetoui*. Sometimes, on land situated at greater altitude, but irrigated artificially, an autumn crop, called *nili*, could be grown.

The great heat made the job of the farm-workers very hard indeed. For that reason they would never go to the fields without a gourd of fresh water. which they would hang in the shade on a nearby tree. Sometimes, if several men were working together. they would take along a small keg of water.

AN INGENIOUS IDEA

In numerous engravings we see monkeys at work picking fruit; they can be seen climbing up the fruit trees and then handing the fruit down to the gardeners. These delightful helpmates most probably diverted a part of their harvest to their own advantage, thus satisfying a perfectly legitimate greed.

We can see in this phenomenon additional proof of the Egyptian's mastery of the art of training animals. Monkeys, in particular, were often put to work. They sometimes carried the torches at a dinner-party; in one of the tomb-paintings, one of them can be seen tossing his flaming torch into the midst of a startled assembly of guests.

ADVANCED POULTRY-BREEDERS

"What most excites our wonder, adds Diodorus and deserves the greatest praise, is the industry shown by the rearers of fowls and geese, who, not contented with the course of natural procreation known in other countries, hatch an infinite number of birds by an artificial process. Dispensing with the incubation of the hens, they with their own hands bring the eggs to maturity; and the young chickens thus produced are not inferior in any respect to those hatched by natural means."

This artificial contrivance has been handed down to modern times, and continues to be employed by the modern inhabitants of Egypt, particularly the Copts, who may be considered to have the best claim to the title of descendants of the ancient Egyptians. The custom is for the proprietors of the ovens to make the round of the villages in the vicinity, to collect the eggs from the peasants, and to give them in charge to the rearers, who, without any previous examination, place all they receive on mats strewn with bran, in a room about 11 feet square, with a flat roof, and about 4 feet in height, over which is another chamber of the same size, with a vaulted roof, and about 9 feet high.

The poulterers may be divided into two classes,—the rearers, and those who sold poultry in the market; the former living in the country and villages, and the latter in the market towns. They fed them for the table; and, regardless of the number required for private consumption, a great many were exclusively fattened for the service of the temple, as well as for the sacred animals, and for the daily rations of the priests and soldiers.

8. CLASSES AND TRADES

THE CASTES

The riches of Egypt were derived mainly from taxes, foreign tribute, monopolies, commerce, mines and, above all, from the production of a fruitful soil. The wants of the poorer classes were easily satisfied. Diodorus wrote that "the Egyptians bring up their children at an incredibly small expense, both in food and clothing, the mildness of the climate enabling them to go without shoes, or indeed without any other clothing." We may assume, therefore, that the yearly bill for shoes and all articles of dress pressed very lightly on the purses of parents in many classes of society. The Egyptians did not suffer from any severe class distinctions, at least not in this particular field. An abundance of grain, herbs and edible plants provided an ample supply of food to the inhabitants of the Nile valley, at a trifling expense and with little labour; and so much corn was produced in this fertile country that, after sufficing for the consumption of a large population, it offered a great surplus for the foreign market; and the quantity on hand enabling the peasant to sell it at a low rate necessarily brought considerable profit to the Government, being exported to other countries, or sold to the traders who visited Egypt for commercial purposes.

In a country thus favoured by Nature, there was no proletariat, and no class struggle; yet the populace was far from enjoying the opulence and luxury to which the upper classes had access. A great difference prevailed between rich and poor, at all levels: housing, dress, food, behaviour and even in the last abode of all, the tomb.

Obedience, even submission, was the rule for the less privileged. Discipline was severe, and exemplary punishments were very strictly codified, out of a desire to treat the people with a rigorous but benevolent paternalism. And it was for this reason that no-one complained.

However, under foreign occupation, under the Persian despots and the iron heel of the Ptolemies, feelings of constraint, dissent and revolt came into being.

Left, the workkshop of a weaver.
Above, a wooden hammer.

The trouble was that the non-indigenous dynasties proved unable to install a purely Egyptian spirit of law, one which complied with what was, admittedly, a very localized form of justice.

PRIESTS, SCRIBES AND WARRIORS

The three great classes of society, priests, scribes and warriors, were by no means castes in the sense of hereditary succession; for though a son often followed the profession of his father, owing to habit, thoughts, education, or patronage and connection, which have existed at all times and in all countries, these three orders were not so distinct from each other as in later times.

The priest of a god was often a military or naval commander, exercised the office of scribe, and was invested with the supervision of public works or local government. A general in the army could marry the daughter of a priest, and his children could be scribes, priests, or public officials. It was certainly difficult if not almost impossible for members of the poorer classes of society to elevate themselves to the higher grades.

There is reason to believe that there was a hereditary territorial aristocracy, but even they were re-invested by the sovereign with their lands.

A female porter, craftsmen, and the toolchest of a craftsman. Right-hand page, inside a butcher's shop.

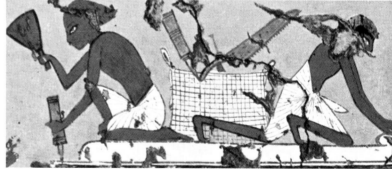

either on account of a kind of feudal tenure, or because the crown was the great landlord of the whole country, and the monarch presented lands to distinguished military officers. Public employments were monopolised by a few great families, considered by some to be an advantageous arrangement of civil government, but the keystone of caste, the limitation of marriage to women of the same order, is unknown to ancient Egypt.

There were therefore no castes, in the strict sense of the term, but there were classes, four of them. Honour to whom honour is due. The first class consisted of the clergy; it included the priests, the soothsayers, judges and even the keepers of the sacred animals.

The agricultural class comprised the farmers, stock-breeders, gardeners, and also the military, huntsmen and sailors.

The third class was that of the town-dwellers: artisans, artists, traders, notaries, public weighers and the various types of scribes.

The fourth class, the least privileged, the poorest and humblest, grouped together the herdsmen, the poultry-keepers, the fishermen, farm labourers and servants.

SOME TRADES

In practice it was difficult to change one's occupation. As Diodorus notes, the members of a given profession or trade constantly rivalled each other in their quest for perfection. Sometimes, it would take several generations to acquire the knack or the special skills peculiar to a given type of job; for this reason shifting jobs was not encouraged. Relying on habit, the sense of custom and tradition, Egyptians generally preferred not to run risks, and therefore chose to stay within the confines of the profession in which they had been raised, the ancestral profession, for their own

personal good and for that of society as a whole.

For this reason, the professions were clearly demarcated, and highly specialized. Encroachments on the preserves of others were resented.

Take the huntsmen, in the second class; they used to accompany the lords on their wild game expeditions. They led the dogs out into the fields, having first trained them. They turned them loose on the trail of the game and made sure that they brought back the slain prey. Sometimes they were self-employed, selling high-quality venison and collecting the bonuses offered for getting rid of pests, such as hyenas and jackals. Another lucrative pastime they indulged in was the ostrich-hunt, as this bird's feathers and eggs were worth their weight in gold.

The function of the public weigher was also a common one. It involved weighing all objects presented to them for a ruling. They would go to people's homes if needed, but they also worked in the streets, setting up their scales temporarily wherever the occasion required. They also set the price of merchandise. They had a reputation for impartiality. Since commerce was largely based on the principle of weighing goods to be exchanged or sold, the weigher had to verify the correct weight each time a transaction took place, and the value of the gold, silver or bronze paid in return was established with reference to this same criterion.

The sailors, although all from the same social class, enjoyed varying fortunes. Rank depended on the post occupied, steersman being held the most important of all. The pilots usually came from the same region; they had to have a perfect knowledge of the bottom of the Nile, as there were no maps—apart from which, everything was altered by the annual inundation.

The boat-builders consisted of carpenters, joiners and wicker-work experts at the same time.

These latter wove the reeds and willow strips which were much used by the fleet. Popular boats were often so light that Strabo emphasized the ease with which they passed the Cataracts—the boatman simply took the boat out of the water and carried it on his back.

Within the class of manufacturers there were several grades, depending on the nature of the job itself and the material used. Weavers, potters and dyers belonged to quite separate branches.

An important part of the lower class was the occupation of brickmaker. These were the people who, working with clay and straw, were quite indispensable to every construction project in Egypt, whether it be a farmhouse or a tomb, as all were made of the untreated brick characteristic of that civilisation. As we have seen, the State created a monopoly so as to keep control of the profits of such a vast economic activity.

A special profession in Egypt was that of the papyrus manufacturer. Here again, the State had a monopoly. In fact, the monopoly of the papyrus in Egypt so increased the price of the commodity, that persons of humble status could not afford to purchase it for ordinary purposes; few documents therefore, are met with written on papyrus, except funeral rituals, the sales of estates, and official papers, which were absolutely required; and so valuable was it, that they frequently obliterated the old writing, and inscribed another document on the same sheet.

For common purposes, pieces of broken pottery, board, and leather were used; an order to visit some monument, a soldier's leave of absence, accounts, and various memoranda, were often written on the fragments of an earthenware vase.

The papyrus makers enjoyed great prestige, and were thus only too happy to pass their trade on to their descendants.

Such were the structures of society, and such they remained. Working conditions were always more or less bearable, and the hierarchy of earnings was accepted. Merit could earn an individual advancement within society, but it was rare. The gods wanted it no other way. And who would complain? Everyone found something for himself in society the way it was, without resentment, without envy and without excessive ambition. And the whole system was crowned, as it were, by religion...

Too much emphasis cannot be laid on the capital role of the scribes in almost every aspect of Egyptian life (figures on left and right). Centre and bottom right, some fine specimens of hieroglyphs. Bottom left, a very interesting model of a study of proportions.

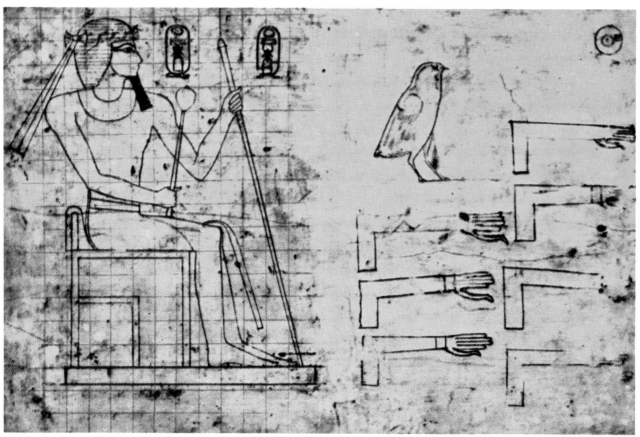

Boats; bottom right, a group of porters.

9. TRANSPORT

NAVIGATION

The Nile made the Egyptians expert boatmen. This river was for them a superb highway, along which both passengers and freight could be moved easily, for the greater benefit of society, as the population, in any case, lived within the narrow band of territory along its banks.

The Nile was navigable throughout the whole length of the Empire. It broadened considerably in the Delta, where it divided into numerous branches, in this particularly heavily populated area. The prevailing winds blew from north to south, against the current. Boatmen thus were able to go downstream easily using their oars, and usually go back up to their point of departure under sail.

Since navigation was overwhelmingly the principal means of transport, the Egyptians built a whole range of practical boats, well adapted to different uses and to the geography and climate.

They varied enormously in size. Some of them were huge. Diodorus mentions one, made of cedar, offered by Sesostris to the gods of Thebes which measured 280 cubits (about 450 feet). Another boat, this time a military vessel, built on the orders of Ptolemy Philopator, was of the same length, but was 75 feet wide and 100 feet high. According to Diodorus it could carry four hundred sailors, four thousand oarsmen and three thousand soldiers. This certainly seems a heavy load, besides which the passengers must have been very cramped!

But there were also more modest craft, sometimes privately owned by a single individual. Some were made of wood, more particularly of a wood "similar", in the words of Herodotus, "to the lotus of Cyrene". Others had a hull made simply of bundles of papyrus fastened together, and were thus very light. This same papyrus also provided much of the equipment, rigging and even

On these pages, the art of Egyptian boats and, facing, a carriage. Below, the making of a papyrus canoe.

sometimes the sails. The keel of these boats was often flat; they could easily be towed along the banks of the river when this proved necessary.

There were some very large freighters, used for transporting grain, stone, bricks and even the gigantic obelisks which were hewn out of a single block in the quarries of Aswan and then carried on the river to the site of the temple, where they were triumphantly erected. There were also tiny one-man punts used for fishing or regular domestic needs. At numerous fixed points along the river there were enormous ferries which provided a regular crossing near major settlements. Ferries also provided a shuttle service across the major canals. There was also a naval fleet, the size of which varied according to the warlike temperament of the Pharaohs. Lastly, the Egyptians also had private pleasure-craft, "yachts" one might say, for the use of the gentry.

These boats, as we have seen, were propelled in many instances through muscle-power—the oarsmen. These used to push the oars instead of pulling them, as we would do today. They usually sat on either side of the boat, on light benches.

Boats were sometimes towed by papyrus ropes from the banks. They could also be propelled punt-style, with a pole—an art at which the Egyptians excelled. But almost all boats had masts, and, as soon as the winds were favourable, which was most of the time, they would hoist the sails. In the bows of the vessel a man would regularly poke the bottom with a long pole: the sandbanks of the Nile were forever changing, and the Egyptians were rightly distrustful for that reason.

The biggest boats had a cabin, often quite tall and commodious; it was usually made of wood, and decorated or painted in bright colours.

CARRIAGES

As masters of the waterways, the Egyptians had few means of transport on land, and were not very expert in this domain.

Their two-wheeled carriages were rudimentary; they were drawn by oxen or horses. The passengers usually stood up; when they sat down, it was on the floor of the vehicle, on a reed mat, with their feet dangling over the side: not a very comfortable means of locomotion. It was a rare luxury to have the carriage covered with a sort of sunshade or a palanquin, as a protection from the rays of the sun.

The more sophisticated of these vehicles had a floor consisting of a web of leather thonging or papyrus rope. The relative elasticity thus provided gave the vehicle a sort of suspension.

The bodywork of the carriage was extremely light; it was situated on the front end and closed only from that side. It was made of wood and strengthened by metal bars or strips of thick leather. The back was completely open, and did not even have a step.

No samples of four-wheeled vehicles have been found. The lightness of the vehicles was such that it was no great burden for the horses. When speed was not essential, the Egyptians sometimes harnessed them to a donkey. Another advantage of this extreme lightness was that, if necessary, a man could carry the vehicle on his back!

10. ADMINISTRATION AND JUSTICE

THE KINGS OF BUREAUCRACY

Whether it was for reasons of temperament, or out of distrust born of a familiarity with the mentality of their peers, Egyptians were extraordinarily cautious. No deal of any sort could be transacted orally. Everything had to be done in writing, following incredibly precise and complicated formalities. As a logical consequence of this state of affairs, Egypt was the kingdom of bureaucracy. A barely credible number of scribes worked in its service.

In the mode of executing deeds, conveyances, and other civil contracts, the Egyptians were peculiarly thorough and meticulous, and the great number of witnesses is a singular feature in those documents. For example, *sixteen* were needed to witness the purchase of a plot of land.

In the times of the Ptolemies, sales of property commenced with a preamble, containing the date of the king in whose reign they were executed; the name of the president of the court, and of the clerk by whom they were written, being also specified. The body of the contract then followed. It stated the name of the individual who sold the land, the description of his person, an account of his parentage, profession, and place of abode; the extend and nature of the land, its situation and boundaries; and concluded with the name of the purchaser, whose parentage and description were also added, and the sum for which it was bought.

But the formalities did not end there. The seller then vouched for his undisturbed possession of it; and, by way of security against any attempt to dispute his title, the name of the other party was inserted as having accepted it, and acknowledged the purchase. The names of witnesses were then affixed; and the president of the court having added his signature, the deed was valid.

Sometimes the seller formally recognised the sale in the following manner:—"All these things have I sold thee: they are thine, I have received their price from thee, and make no demand upon thee for them from this day; and if any person disturb thee in the possession of them, I will withstand the attempt; and, if I do not otherwise repel it, I will use compulsory means," or "I will indemnify thee."

In order more effectually to protect the virtuous and detect the wicked, it was enacted that every one should at certain times present himself before the magistrates or provincial governors, and give his name, his place of abode, his profession or employment, and, in short, the mode in which he gained his livelihood; the particulars being duly registered by the official scribes.

In approaching it was required that the individual should make a profound bow, which was similar to that described by Herodotus, the hand falling down to the knee; and this mark of deference was expected from every one, as a token of respect to the court, on all occasions, both when accused before a magistrate, and when attending at the police office to lodge a complaint, or to vindicate his character from an unjust imputation.

In a deed of the time of Cleopatra Cocce and Ptolemy Alexander I., written in Greek, and relating to the sale of a piece of land at Thebes, the parties are thus described:—"Pamonthes, aged about forty-five, of middle size, dark complexion, and handsome figure, bald, round-faced and straight-

Left, an official and, below, the ubiquitous scribes.

nosed; Snachomneus, aged about twenty, of middle size; sallow complexion, round-faced and straight-nosed; Semmuthis Persineï, aged about twenty-two, of middle size, sallow complexion, round-faced, flat-nosed, and of quiet demeanour; and Tathlyt Persineï, aged about thirty, of middle size, sallow complexion, round face, and straight nose,— the four being children of Petepsais, of the leather-cutters of the Memnonia; and Nechutes the less, the son of Asos, aged about forty, of middle size, sallow complexion, cheerful countenance, long face and straight nose, with a scar upon the middle of his forehead."

These descriptions constituted a genuine individual file, making it possible to issue a passport. Misrepresentation of any piece of information,

Left, details of two statuettes depicting high officials: one is holding a papyrus on his knees and the other is wearing a breast-plate suggestive of high rank.

about the name or profession, for example, could bring severe penalties, including beatings and death.

One would imagine that the Egyptians, a happy nation living in a benign climate, should never have had any debts. But the fondness for luxury sometimes creates artificial needs, and the State had to take measures to legislate in respect of this abominable custom.

The laws changed with the changing times, but the spirit remained the same: the accumulation of debt had to be prevented, and crooks had to be rendered harmless, so that the weak could be protected. Legislators could do this by requiring the drawing up of a written contract.

Usury was in all cases condemned by the Egyptian legislature; and when money was borrowed, even with a written agreement, it was forbidden to allow the interest to increase to more than double the original sum. Nor could the creditors seize the debtor's person: their claims and right were confined to the goods in his possession, and such as were really his own; by this was meant anything which was the produce of his labour, or what he had received from another individual to whom they lawfully belonged.

To prevent the accumulation of debt, and to protect the interests of the creditor, another remarkable law was enacted, which, while it shows how greatly they endeavoured to check the increasing evil, proves the high respect paid by the Egyptians to the memory of their parents, and to the sanctity of their religious ceremonies. By this it was pronounced illegal for anyone to borrow money without giving in pledge the body of his father, or of his nearest relative; and, if he failed to redeem so sacred a deposit, he was considered infamous, and at his death the celebration of the accustomed funeral obsequies was denied him, and he could not enjoy the right of burial either in the tomb of his ancestors, or in any other place of burial; nor could he inter his children, or any of his family, as long as the debt was unpaid, the creditor being put in actual possession of his family tomb. That is, if the debt was not paid within a certain time, the mummy could be removed from the tomb.

We may conclude that the body itself was seldom given up, since possession of the tomb was sufficient, and much less inconvenient to the creditor than to have a stranger's mummy in his living-room.

Laws like these show how far the Egyptians had got into debt, and how drastic were the measures needed to keep them out of it.

JUSTICE

Causes of ordinary occurrence were decided by those who held the office of judges. None were admitted to this post but the most upright and learned individuals; and, in order to make the office more select, and more readily to obtain persons of known character, ten only were chosen from each of the three cities—Thebes, Memphis, and Heliopolis.

According to Diodorus "they formed an assembly which was in no way inferior to the Areopages of Athens or the Senate of Lacedemonia."

These thirty persons made up the magistrature. At their first meeting they elected the most eminent of their own number to serve as president, with the title of Grand Judge. Since his role was the most important, his salary was also, logically, higher. In order to replace him on the assembly of magistrates, his home town was entitled to appoint another thirtieth judge.

All of them were very well paid. It was felt that they should be rich enough to maintain a standard of living above the ordinary, in keeping with their elevated rank and responsibilities; in this way they would presumably be safe from temptations and corruption. In return, they were expected to show great diligence and care and to administer justice soundly and efficiently.

As Diodorus shows, the Egyptian laws were not designed merely to arouse men's feelings about the prospect of distant rewards or punishments, nor to threaten the possibility of divine vengeance. They were, on the contrary, immediate in their effect.

Besides impartiality and the principle whereby each case should be treated according to its merits, another important feature of justice in ancient Egypt was the fact that it was administered free of charge. In spirit, the Egyptian laws sought to give protection to those who were really in need of it.

At the beginning of the trial the president of the court put on the emblem of truth and the eight volumes of the Egyptian laws were brought before him for his guidance. Then the plaintiff stated his case in writing, listing in detail all aspects of the alleged injury or offence.

The defendant then wrote his answer to each of the plaintiff's charges, either rejecting the accusations made against him, or trying to reduce their gravity. The plaintiff replied in writing, and, after the accused had made a second statement in his defence, the papers were given to the judges. In the absence of witnesses, they issued their verdict on the strength of the depositions made by the parties alone. The opinion of the judges then had to be ratified by the president, who ruled definitively on the case: he did so by touching the winning party with the figure of truth. It was felt that the cause of justice would be better served by this method than by the hearing or impassioned, eloquent pleas by rival advocates, since, in the view of the ancient Egyptians, eloquence frequently had the effect of fascinating the mind, and tending to throw a veil over guilt and to pervert truth. The persuasive arguments of oratory, or those artifices which move the passions and excite the sympathy of the judges, were avoided, and thus neither did an appeal to their feelings, nor the tears and dissimulation of an offender, soften the just rigour of the laws. And while ample time was afforded to each party to make or to disprove an accusation, no opportunity was given to the offender to take advantage of his opponent, but poor and rich, ignorant and learned, honest and dishonest, were placed on a equal footing; and it was the case, rather than the persons, upon which the judgement was passed.

The Egyptians felt that truth or justice were the principal civic virtues, because they involved one's fellow-citizens directly. They therefore taught the young to appreciate and nurture this quality. Lies were considered as being not only a monstrous and dishonourable offence, but they could also entail legal action, if a tort could be proved. Severe punishment was inflicted on anyone who slandered a dead person, while a false witness incurred the same penalty as the offender himself. Perjury was a crime against the gods, a violation of one's word, which was punishable by death.

PUNISHMENTS

The laws and regulations were intended not only for the lower classes, but also for those at the pinnacle of society, including the Pharaoh, who willingly complied, as Diodorus observes, with the rules of public and private life. This applied even to his choice of food and drink.

The Pharaohs, just like the lowliest of their subjects, were supposed to be just. When the vizir, or supreme magistrate, was appointed, he was read the following exhortation: "The height of the divine abomination would be to show bias. These, then, are your instructions: you shall treat those you do not know exactly as you would treat those you do know, and those who live near you just as you would those who live far away... Beware, because you will keep this post only so long as you stay within its prerogatives!"

The deliberate killing of a free man or even a slave was punishable by death, regardless of the social status of the culprit. Complicity in murder and failure to help a person in danger was also blows were inflicted in both cases by men.

Capital punishment usually took the form of

punished severely. In case of theft, witnesses were supposed to do everything they could to stop the wrongdoer; if they were found guilty of negligence in this respect they were sentenced to be whipped and also to be denied food for three full days.

The prerogative of the royal pardon could be exercised on behalf of the guilty party; penalties were thus sometimes commuted by royal decreee.

The murder of a child was considered an odious crime; fathers had no right of life or death over their offspring. The guilty father was not, however, executed, as it was thought contradictory to take away the life of the one who had given it to the child. The punishment chosen was one likely to induce remorse and grief: the body of the dead child was tied to the guilty father for three full days.

Parricide was also severely punished: the offender was condemned to be lacerated with reeds, thrown onto brambles and then burnt alive.

The stick was inflicted on both sexes, but it was not administered in the same position: men and boys were given it lying down, bound hand and foot, while women remained seated, though the hanging, though beheading was also practised occasionally. While in prison, criminals were kept bound. Prisoners on trial were kept in the house of the chief of police.

The law of retaliation also existed: forgers, falsifiers of weights and measures, makers of counterfeit seals, unscrupulous scribes had their hands—or hand, as the case may be—chopped off.

THEFT

Theft, trickery and minor offences were punished with a beating, but breaking and entering sometimes carried the death penalty. Diodorus mentions a highly original monarch named Actisanes who instituted a curious form of punishment: he had thieves' noses cut off, and then banished them to a remote desert place, where they built a town which, according to Pliny, was called Rhinonolura ("no nose"), in keeping with the appearance of those who built it. In this way criminals were removed from society and punished at the same time, the innocent were protected, and useful work was done.

It is thought, however, that there was a custom which was distinctly less moral than those we have been considering. Egyptians were fond of theft and also good at it. And the punishments were not always much of a deterrent. Certain robbers, therefore, apparently formed a secret league to carry on their anti-social activities. They elected a chief, who was kept informed of all the robberies committed by the members of the society, the amount taken, the nature of the loot, the name and profession of the victim.

It happened that the victim, by devious means, sometimes made it known that he would like his property back, in return for a substantial fee and a promise not to institute proceedings. This sort of assurance would be advantageous even if it did not involve the punishment of the guilty party. At least the property was returned, which did not always happen when the courts took a hand.

Not all thefts appeared on the list of the chief of the league. In such cases, the offending thief was an outsider, whose private operations could only be harmful to the profession as a whole. Of course, he would be tracked down, punished and... taxed.

Above, a scene of childbirth and, below, surgical instruments. The fine statue on the right is that of a female healer.

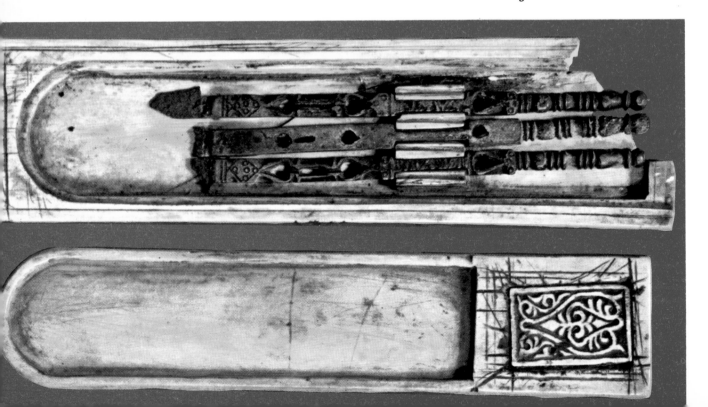

11. MEDICINE AND DOCTORS

DOCTORS

Being highly practical by nature, the Egyptians invented medicine, a notably useful and pragmatic discipline. Their primacy in this field was undisputed.

The care which the Egyptians took of their health was a source of astonishment for foreign observers, particularly Greeks and Romans. Herodotus comments on "the very particular concern of those living in the corn country for their health". Pliny thought that the large number of doctors meant that the population of Egypt suffered from a great number of diseases – a paradoxical piece of logic. Herodotus, on the other hand, thought that there was no healthier nation than the Egyptians.

At any rate, they really tried to do something about illness, and had a large medical corps to help them.

Egyptian doctors had a special status. After being authorized to practise their art, on completion of certain prescribed studies, they were officially approved and received a salary, like any other civil servant. They could be summoned at any moment and had to provide care for the needy free of charge. Yet they could also charge fees. Naturally, they were under State supervision. If their patients failed to get better, or died, the State could enquire into the reasons for such a failure, and make sure that the doctor had followed the rules of his art. Diodorus thought that these rules were based on the belief that tradition and past experience were the safest guarantee of any therapy. Therefore, if the remedies had been administered in keeping with the norms, the doctor was acquitted. Woe betide any doctor who had taken any unsuccessful initiative! He could find himself in real trouble, and even risk capital punishment. One has to admit that such a system does little to encourage progress.

Egyptians were convinced dietitians, and took immense care with their food. As a preventive measure, they practised fasting, abstinence and purgations.

However, if these precautions failed to prevent sickness, they turned to medicine. The Edwin Smith papyrus—named after the American scholar who acquired it—is a work dealing with the treatment of injuries, and shows just how serious such studies were.

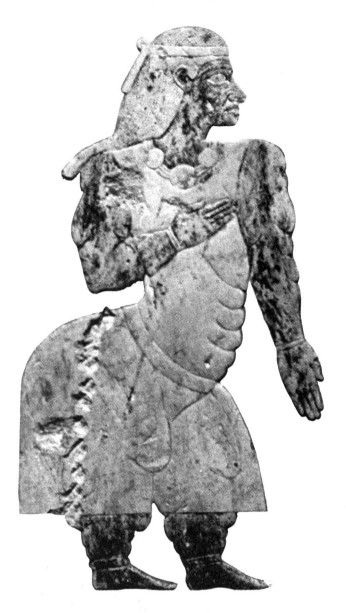

A fat woman.

broken bones. Perfectly healed fractures can be seen in numerous mummies.

The Ebers papyrus—named for the same reason as the preceding one—also deals with surgery, but it is above all a manual for the teaching of anatomy and pharmacy.

It studies the blood, the heart and the nerves, and gives recipes for many remedies, such as plasters, balms and ointments, of vegetable, mineral and also animal origin. The ingredients were sometimes crushed, and sometimes boiled or blended; they could be sifted through a piece of fabric, diluted with clear water, beer, wine, oil, or milk. Medicinal plants were well known; dozens of them were used, the commonest being castor oil. Homer, in the Odyssey, describes the many valuable medicines given by Polydamna, the wife of Thonis, to Helen, while in Egypt, "a country whose fertile soil produces an infinity of drugs, some salutary and some pernicious".

Each temple had a full-scale laboratory, where medications were made and stocked.

The most famous of the Egyptian doctors was Herophilus, the pioneer of the science of anatomy. He persuaded Pharaoh Ptolemy to let him perform not merely autopsies, but also, apparently, live experiments and research on certain criminals who were made available to him. In this way he was able to study very seriously all aspects of anatomy; he had—for the period in which he lived —a very thorough knowledge of the eye, the liver, the heart, and the brain.

Egyptian doctors suffered, however, from an extreme degree of specialization. Herodotus points out that "they could practise no branch other than their own". He quotes examples, such as the oculist, the dentist, the doctor who was allowed to treat only intestines or only the head, etc., Childbirth was the exclusive province of the midwives; doctors could not be involved at all. He sees in that a sign of scientific advancement, and the result of truly profound knowledge. But we are inclined to disagree.

At any rate, Egyptian medicine was immeasurably superior to that of any other nation of the same period. Its renown spread far and wide beyond its own frontiers; the king of Persia would hear of no other, and people would come to Egypt from Syria and Assyria for consultations.

This papyrus examines 48 cases: dislocations, wounds and fractures resulting from accidents, starting with those affecting the head, and gradually going down the body to the lower limbs.

The diagnosis was established after extraordinarily precise observations had been made. In conclusion it proposed three possibilities: a doctor could act with full success, he could try, with some chances of success, or he stood no chance at all, in which case he should do nothing.

The techniques were numerous and varied. Fractures were properly set, splints were applied, and wounds were sutured. There was a sort of adhesive plaster which worked wonders with

128

Left, a picture of some surgical instruments.
Below, example of the kind of case used to carry these instruments.

MEDICINE AND SUPERSTITION

We should not forget, however, that in Egypt sickness, like health, was first and foremost the work of the gods. This meant that medicine was, *ipso facto,* linked to religion.

When a person was sick, it was because evil spirits, sent by hostile powers, were inhabiting his body and pouring poison into it. Getting better meant ridding oneself of these spirits, by acting on those who had sent them in the first place. Doctors were thus scientists, magicians· and priests, at the same time.

Magic was always present in any treatment, and the remedies were viewed as potions. Any cure was accompanied by ritual words and gestures, invocations and imprecations. Offerings were also made: certain patients promised a sum of money for the maintenance of the sacred animals, others made votive offerings, or gave jewels and works of art. If the patient was a child, the gift had to weigh the same as the child's hair which had been shaved off for the occasion. An image of the afflicted organ was often hung up in the temple, by way of thanks. For example, ears, noses, arms or eyes could be seen, in rows, in the temple. Some people chose to have an inscription made of some votive phrase expressing the gratitude of the former patient.

Provident Egyptians sometimes asked the gods for good health for themselves and their families, as a preventive measure. They would first assure the gods of the profound respect they felt for them, and then they would ask for the divine protection. To avoid all confusion, the applicant for divine favours would give his precise name, the amount of the offering and the date when it was made. The names of those to whom the benign influence of the gods was to be extended were also inscribed.

Medicine was all well and good, but it would be nothing if the gods so decided.

This practice was extremely common; from gullible peasants and sophisticated lords alike, the gifts were piled up high at the feet of the images of the gods. These pleas were often addressed to local gods, but also to Isis, the protector of childhood, to Nephtys, her sister, who was specially good to women, or to Horus, the falcon-headed god who carried in his hand the *ankh,* or symbol of life. But Osiris also received a considerable

share of the homage, being the god of regeneration.

As one might expect. this custom. which greatly swelled the revenues of the temples. could not fail to be encouraged by the priests and the keepers of the temples. Everyone, both sick and healthy. was thus constantly kept in mind of the advantages of divine help, and invited to avail themselves of it in return for a modest material contribution.

Dreams were thought to be another source of information about a person's health. They were viewed as a premonition. The gods could also send indications, in the form of dreams. about the manner of treating a certain condition. Generally speaking, the Egyptians had a deep and fearful respect for dreams.

The painting shown below depicts a doctor receiving gifts in return for his professional attention.

12. RELIGION AND BELIEFS

A SUPERSTITIOUS PEOPLE

Egyptians were superstitious. In all circumstances, whether it be marriage, the construction of a house or an important decision, they never failed to consult the omens.

Depending on the day on which a child was born prophecies were made about its entire future. The signs influenced the handling of pending business. The entrails of animals suggested to the priests the nature of future events.

Herodotus noticed the immense care with which the Egyptians watched for the omens: "When any event occurs, they note it down in writing, recording carefully all the consequences which follow from it". And if, later. a similar event occurred. they inferred that it would be followed by the same effects.

They even, says Plutarch, "look upon children as gifted with a kind of faculty of divination, and they are ever anxious to observe the accidental prattle they talk during play, especially if it be in a sacred place, deducing from it presages of future events." Omens were frequently drawn from common accidents, as tokens of good and bad luck.

Perfectly casual incidents were often regarded as signs of failure of good luck: for example. when the engineer in charge of the transport of a monolithic shrine from Elephantine to Sais breathed a sigh, it was sufficient to bring the whole operation to a halt and to prevent him from entering the holy place to receive it.

Sacrifices of animals. offerings, libations and the use of incense were all exceedingly ancient practices.

THE PRIESTS

The universal respect in which the priests were held was based on their exclusive right to regulate all spiritual matters, and to announce the will. threaten the wrath and supervise the worship of the gods, as well as on the superior knowledge to which they alone, by virtue of their education, had access. In return for their services to State and people, they were awarded a high income and numerous gifts, in keeping with their elevated social rank and the sacred nature of their duties.

We may safely assume that the priests, like the

other members of the social élite, enjoyed quite a high standard of living, which was deemed compatible with their wisdom, with their external appearance of self-denial and their virtue. They certainly set a worthy example through their own conduct, their practice of abstinence, and their general morality, though the stark contrast between their wealth and that of the ordinary populace does strike a jarring note.

Respect for the priesthood was also induced by the importance of the posts they held on major State occasions: and the superior abilities of that powerful body gave it ample means of establishing its authority over credulous and superstitious minds. The priesthood took a prominent part in everything; there was no ceremony in which they did not participate, and even military regulations were subject to the influence of the sacerdotal

caste. Nothing was beyond their jurisdiction: the king himself was subject to the laws established by them for his conduct, and even for his mode of living.

If the priests were anxious to establish a character for learning and piety, they were not less so in their efforts to impress by their outward demeanour, and to set a proper example of humility and self-denial; and if not in their houses, at least in their mode of living, they were remarkable for simplicity and abstinence. They committed no excesses either in eating or drinking; their food was plain and in a stated quantity, and wine was used at all times in strict moderation. And so fearful were they lest the body should not "sit light upon the soul", and excess should cause a tendency to increase "the corporeal man", that they paid a scrupulous attention to the most trifling details of dict.

particulars of diet.

They were not only scrupulous about the quantity, but the quality of their food; and certain viands were alone allowed to appear at table. Above all meats, pork, was particularly obnoxious; and fish both of the sea and the Nile were forbidden them, though so generally eaten by the rest of the Egyptians.

Given the sacred nature of their functions, they were obliged to undergo frequent and strict purifications, even going so far as to eat no salt with their meals. However, they were always allowed to eat certain vegetables, which were felt to be good for the health.

They were quite as severe in their ablutions. They had to perform all sorts of rites. They had to bathe twice a day and twice a night. For those whose standards of purity were even higher, it was possibly to bathe only in the water from which the ibis drank—and which was thus certainly free from pollution.

Apart from that, they shaved their heads and their whole bodies once every three days and spared no effort to ensure the cleanliness of their persons. A great ceremony of purification was held just before the major feasts.

Certain women from eminent families devoted themselves to the service of the god of Thebes. They contributed to most of the ceremonies and wore emblems indicating their rank. These women were the daughters of nobles and princesses, in fact, and it was an honour for them to perform these tasks.

CEREMONIES

Though the priests were aware of the nature of their gods, and all those who understood the mysteries of the religion looked upon the Divinity as a sole and undivided Being, the people, not admitted to participation in those important secrets, were left in perfect ignorance respecting the objects they were taught to adore; and every one was not only permitted, but encouraged, to believe in the real sanctity of the idol, and the actual existence of the god whose figure he beheld. The bull Apis was by them deemed as sacred and as worthy of actual worship as the Divinity of which it was the type; similarly other emblems were substituted for the deities they represented.

Even when the cult of Râ had become the official form of worship, the priests kept their local divinities, and the populace was not in the least disturbed by such theological contradictions.

THE MYSTERIES

One has to realize that Egyptian religion was esoteric in nature, and that the clergy was based on a strict hierarchy. At the lowest level were the popular beliefs. Beyond those, and in direct proportion to their rank, the priests were initiated into the mysteries, which were truly understood only by the very highest dignitaries.

As Clement of Alexandria says: "The Egyptians neither entrusted their mysteries to everyone, nor degraded the secrets of divine matters by disclosing them to the profane, reserving them for the heir apparent of the throne, and for such of the priests as excelled in virtue and wisdom."

From all we can learn on the subject, it appears that the mysteries consisted of two degrees, denominated the greater and the less; and in order to become qualified for admission into the higher class, it was necessary to have passed through those of the inferior degree; and each of them was probably divided into ten different grades. It was necessary that the character of the candidate for initiation should be pure and unsullied; and novitiates were commanded to study those lessons which tended to purify the mind and to encourage morality. The honour of ascending from the less to the greater mysteries was as highly esteemed as it was hard to obtain: no ordinary qualification was required of the aspirant to this important privilege; and, apart from enjoying an acknowledged reputation for learning and morality, he was required to undergo the most severe ordeal, and to show the greatest moral resignation.

Rare indeed were those from outside the priesthood who succeeded in being initiated. And they were rarer still if they were foreigners. Even so, certain Greeks, during the reign of the Ptolemies, were successful.

THE SACRED ANIMALS

The first Egyptians, like all other peoples with incipient religions, deified the marvels of Nature, in particular, the essential qualities of the animals which surrounded them—the ferocity of the lion, or the strength of the crocodile. The first divinities were also animal.

For example, Kroun, the god associated with the mysteries of creation was a ram, noted for his pacifism. Thoueris, god of generation and fertility, was a hippopotamus. Thot, the divinity of wisdom and knowledge, and for that reason patron of the scribes, was depicted by an ibis or a baboon, doubtless because of the serious poses that animal can adopt.

Even when, before the first dynasty, religion assumed an anthropomorphic character, Egyptians found it hard to part with their ancestral beliefs. They worshipped hybrid deities: Thot kept the head of an ibis on a man's body; Anubis, the god of the dead, became a man with a jackal's head. Note, in this latter case, the paradoxical nature of this image: jackals were known to unearth the dead while Anubis, on the contrary, was supposed to watch over their eternal rest.

It is true that there was some sort of obscure but symptomatic link between these images and totemism. Living specimens of sacred animals were adored and honoured. Their bodies were sometimes even mummified. At Kom-Ombo, for example, a large number of crocodiles have been found surrounded by bandages. Animal worship increased, moreover, as the Empire declined.

Just as the worship of deities changed from one region to another, the animals worshipped were not the same everywhere, any more than those offered in sacrifice. The Mendesians, who offered sacrificial sheep, would not sacrifice goats, whereas the Thebans did exactly the opposite.

The arbitrary choice of peculiar emblems, and the adoration paid to animals and inanimate objects, frequently depended upon accident, or some peculiar local 'reason: and though great respect was shown to the ichneumon, from its destroying the eggs of the crocodile, in places where that animal was considered an enemy of man, it obtained no honours in those where the crocodile was a sacred animal, as the type of a beneficent deity. But if, in most instances, the motives assigned for their choice appear capricious and unsatisfactory, we frequently discover some plausible pretext derived from a sanitary notion, as in the case of their abstinence from pork, beans and certain fish of the Nile.

In order to ensure that these prescriptions were put into effect, the prohibitions were declared to be sacred in origin. As Pophyrus puts it: remarks: "Either the Egyptians felt that animals were really gods, or they showed their gods with the heads of oxen, birds or other creatures so that people would abstain from eating them, as they did with human flesh, or for other, more mysterious reasons." Perhaps; but we are still none the wiser.

At any rate, with time, the original reason was forgotten, and it yielded to blind adoration. But Plutarch tells us that "it is evident that the religious rites and ceremonies were never based on mere myths or superstitions; they were created with the aim of promoting the morality and the happiness of those whose duty it was to respect them."

THE SACRED APIS BULL

The Egyptians not only paid divine honours to the Apis bull, but, considering him the living image and representative of Osiris, they consulted him as an oracle, and drew from his actions good or bad omens. They were in the habit of offering him any kind of food, with the hand; if he took it, the answer was considered favourable; if he refused, it was thought to be a sinister omen.

Pausanias says that those who wished to consult Apis first burnt incense on an altar, filling the lamps with oil which were lighted there, and depositing a piece of money on the altar to the right of the statue of the god. Then placing their mouth near his ear, in order to consult him, they asked what ever question they wished. This done, they withdrew covering their two ears until they were outside the sacred precincts of the temple; and there listening to the first expression anyone said they drew from it the desired omen.

On the whole, the sacred animal rarely left one of the two stables where he was kept. Sometimes he had access to an adjacent yard where he could be visited. When he moved about he was escorted by numerous guards, who cleared a path for him through the crowd and prevented ordinary mortals from coming too close. A choir of children singing hymns in his honour went ahead of the procession.

DEATH AND JUDGMENT

As soon as the sad news of someone's death became known, all the friends of the deceased met at his house and joined the family in a lavish display of emotion. They would run through the streets weeping and moaning loudly as they went, they would throw dust over themselves and wander throughout the town as if seized by a mad despair.

The family continued scenes of this sort for the seventy-two days during which the body was in the custody of the embalmer. Mourning was a serious affair: no pleasure or amusement of any sort was allowed. They wore dark, modest clothes, avoided luxury or finery of any sort, and even went without shaving, and almost, even, without washing. In order to pay tribute to the dead person, one had to show one's grief as vividly as possible.

Once the body had been embalmed, it was returned to the family. It could either be simply wrapped in bandages, or placed in one or several sarcophagi. The splendour of the decorations and the number of sarcophagi obviously depended on how much the family could afford. Sometimes the dead person himself had previously set aside an amount for his funeral. The sarcophagi fitted into each other successively, and they could be beautifully decorated and gilded.

Then one had to prepare for the funeral ceremony. There were two possibilities. In the first of these, the family decided not to part with their loved one immediately, and to keep the body at home. This was often the wish of the spouse; and the widower or the widow would wait, in the same house, until they themselves died, so that a joint funeral could take place.

In such cases the sarcophagus was placed upright in one room of the house, solidly leaning against the strongest wall. For those who could afford there was also the possibility of building another room, next to the house, in which the coffin could be kept.

Even when burial was chosen, this being the second possibility, the funeral might take place several months after the embalming. The deceased was in no hurry, and was, in any case, well prepared for a long wait. The tomb had to be made ready; and even if it had been ordered before the death, various inscriptions or some additional paintings might still have to be added. Sometimes people bought an existing tomb, but then time had to be allowed for modifications.

When burial was chosen, the sarcophagus was placed on a hearse standing on a sleigh, and was taken to the banks of the lake of the *nome* (region). Each major town had its own lake, because funerals were best held at the water's edge.

The real ceremony took place there: the dead person was to be judged. His friends spoke of his early years, and gave an account of the main stages of his life. They praised his virtues, his piety, temperance, tolerance or goodness. Sometimes, however, accusations were made against him. If they were very grave, the clergy could refuse burial. This was particularly the case if the deceased had incurred debts which the family could not—or would not—pay.

In such circumstances, all his kin felt great shame and resentment. The duration of this prohibition depended, like any sentence, on the gravity of the offence or the wrong that had been done. Admittedly, a few offerings quietly made to the servants of religion would do much to soften the severity of the clergy. Yet its reputation was too important for it to allow a great injustice to be committed. Charges of prevarication were never known to have been levelled against the clergy.

The curious photograph on the left is of a child's mummy.
Below, a group of weeping women on a funeral boat.

A TERRIBLE DISGRACE

The disgrace of being condemned at this public ordeal was in itself a strong inducement to every one to abstain from crime: not only was there the fear of leaving a bad name, but the dread of exposure.

It was not ordinary individuals alone who were subjected to a public ordeal at their death: the character of the king himself was doomed to undergo the same test; and if anyone could establish proofs of his impiety or injustice, he was denied the usual funeral obsequies when in the presence of the assembled multitude his body was brought to be sacred lake, or, as Diodorus states, to the vestibule of the tomb. "The customary trial having commenced, anyone was permitted to present himself as an accuser. The pontiffs first passed an encomium upon his character, enumerating all his noble actions, and pointing out the merit of each; to which the people, who were assembled to the number of several thousands, if they felt those praises to be just, responded with favourable acclamations. If on the other hand, his life had been stained with vice or injustice, they showed their dissent by loud murmurs: and several instances are recorded of Egyptian monarchs having been deprived of the honour of the customary public funeral by the opposing voice of the people." "The effect of this," adds the historian, "was that succeeding kings, fearing so disgraceful a censure after death, and the eternal stigma attached to it, studied by their virtuous conduct to deserve the good opinion of their subjects; and it could not fail to be a great incentive to virtue, independent of the feelings arising from a wish to deserve the gratitude of men, and the fear of forfeiting the favour of the gods."

Each major town, like Thebes or Memphis, and even each provincial capital had its lake, and the funeral procession had to go there. Even when the priests granted a dispensation, to allow the body be taken to another town, as was sometimes done for those who wished to be buried at Abydos or some other privileged place, the ceremony of judgment had to be held on the shores of the lake of the city of origin.

Those persons who, from their extreme poverty, had no place prepared for receiving their body when denied the privilege of passing the sacred

lake, appear to have been interred on the shores they were forbidden to leave; archeologists have found the bones of many buried near the site of the lake of Thebes, which appeared to be of bodies imperfectly preserved, as of persons who could not afford the more expensive processes of embalming.

A MODEST FUNERAL

Most of the time, funerals were held simply, the procession consisting of the family, friends, and priests. The hearse was drawn on a sleigh by two or three oxen. Several men helped the animals by pulling on a rope.

The priest accompanied the procession, burning incense and pouring libations as he went. He was dressed in a leopard-skin mantle. He later performed the sacrifice. Behind him came an official of lower rank, dressed in a full, simple tunic which came down to his knees. It was made of a stiff, coarse fabric, very similar to the *abbaieh*. He help out in front of him a long taper. In front of the hearse walked a woman clasping one arm with her other hand as a sign of grief, her hair bound up in a fillet, her breasts bare and her dress held in place by a strap passing over her shoulder. She sometimes wore a scarf around her hips. She acted as an official mourner.

This kind of procession was the kind which followed the coffin of a man of modest rank, artisan, man of the people or scribe of weights and measures; however, the lavishness deployed on such occasions depended on how much the family could afford.

In any case, Egyptians wanted to do their utmost to have the finest possible funeral and tomb that their means would allow.

EMBALMING

The account given by Diodorus is similar to that of the historian of Halicarnassus. "The funerals of the Egyptians are conducted upon three different scales,—the most expensive, the more moderate, and the humblest. The first is said to cost a talent of silver; the second twenty-two minæ; and the third is extremely cheap. The persons who embalm the bodies are artists who have learnt this secret from their ancestors. They present to the friends of the deceased who apply to them an estimate of the funeral expenses, and ask them in what manner they wish it to be performed; which being agreed upon, they deliver the body to the proper persons appointed to the office. First, one, who is denominated the scribe, marks upon the left side of the body, as it lies on the ground, the extent of the incision which is to be made; then another, who is called *paraschistes*, cuts open as much of the flesh as the law permits with an Ethiopian stone, and immediately runs away, pursued by those who are present, throwing stones at him amidst bitter execrations, as if to cast upon him all the odium of this necessary act. For they look upon everyone who has offered violence to, or inflicted a wound or any other injury upon a human body, to be hateful; but the embalmers, on the contrary, are held in the greatest consideration and respect, being the associates of the priests, and permitted free access to the temples as sacred persons.

"As soon as they have met together to embalm the body thus prepared for them, one introduces his hand through the aperture into the abdomen, and takes everything out, except the kidneys and heart. Another cleanses each of the viscera with palm wine and aromatic substances. Lastly, after having applied oil of cedar and other things to the whole body for upwards of *thirty* days, they add myrrh, cinnamon, and other drugs, which have not only the power of preserving the body for a length of time, but of imparting to it a fragrant odour. It is then restored to the friends of the deceased."

So perfectly were the bodies preserved that the eyebrows and eyelashes remained unchanged, and the features easily recognizable, so that the family and friends felt they still had the living person before them. For that reason they sometimes chose to keep the mummy in their own house.

RITES AND MUMMIES

The offerings made to the dead were similar to the ordinary oblations in honour of the gods. It was not to the deceased as a man transferred to the order of the gods that these ceremonies performed, but to that particular portion of the divine essence which constituted the soul of each individual and returned to the Deity after death.

Everyone, therefore whose virtuous life entitled him to admission into the regions of the blessed, was supposed to be again united to the Deity, of whom he was an emanation; and, with the emblem of Ma, purporting to show that he was judged or justified, he received the holy name of Osiris. His body was so bound up as to resemble the mysterious ruler of Amenti; it bore some of the emblems peculiar to him, and the beard of a form which belonged exclusively to the gods was given to the deceased to show that he had assumed the character of that deity.

After the funeral, offerings were also offered to the god Osiris, on behalf of the deceased and certain services or liturgies were celebrated at the family's expense.

If the deceased had relatives or children who

were priests, these latter were entitled to officiate. The ceremonies involved a sacrifice made, on behalf of the deceased, to one or several gods. such as Osiris, Anubis or others related to Amenti. Incense and libations were also offered. A prayer was read in the presence of the family and friends. All of them gave free rein to the grief they felt on the death of their loved one.

The priest who officiated was chosen from the higher ranks of the priesthood, the only ones who were authorized to wear the leopard-skin mantle. But the other rituals were celebrated by priests of lower rank.

The service was sometimes held long after the burial; it could be repeated at given intervals for months on end—as long as the family footed the bill.

When the mummy was to remain in the house, it was placed in a transportable wooden niche, with folding doors. The niche was carried on the sleigh at the same time as the hearse.

The Egyptians invited to the funeral made the usual offerings of incense, libations, cakes, flowers and fruit. Sometimes the mummy was anointed with scented oil. A parchment scroll was deposited next to the body, listing the ritual which had been followed. The functions of the different clerics were based on a most elaborate hierarchy.

And that included another privilege, of some significance: only the clergy was entitled to deal in tombs...

Clients sometimes preferred to buy a ready-made tomb, which had merely to be touched up with a bit of paint, some inscriptions and a few figurines, representing the deceased, for that "personal" touch.

The paintings showed scenes from the life of the dead person; each scene illustrates the importance of family life. Husband and wife are seen with their arms around each other's neck, with their children nearby. But since this aspect was the same on all tomb paintings, these scenes did not have to be changed when this final resting-place changed hands.

As happened in all Egyptian transactions, the sale of a tomb, the accessories needed for the ceremony, the services rendered by the priests were all the subject of protracted discussions. Great bargaining skill was exhibited by all concerned. These transactions thus took a long time, and it was necessary to choose one's moment to do a deal.

Once matters were settled, a deed was carefully drawn up, assuring the buyer of guaranteed ownership. Here again, the requisite number of witnesses was duly recorded and observed.

Tombs had upper chambers covered with paintings, and one or more cellars, between twenty and seventy feet long, along the sides of which alcoves were hewn out of the rock. Each of these spaces could accommodate one coffin.

After burial, the cellar was closed with masonry, but it could always be opened up again whenever another member of the family died.

The upper chamber, which was so beautifully decorated with paintings, was more a monument in honour of the deceased, than a true tomb. It served as a reception room for friends attending the services there.

Each tomb had a door, with one or two panels turning on hinges and closed with bolts, bars and locks. Lastly, as described by Herodotus, with reference to the precautions taken to protect the treasury of Rhampsinitus, the tomb was closed with a clay seal bearing inscriptions about the deceased.

The congregation then went to eat a meal at which they enjoyed all the good things normally found at such receptions.

And why not? In all countries in the world, funeral orations directly precede a fine meal!

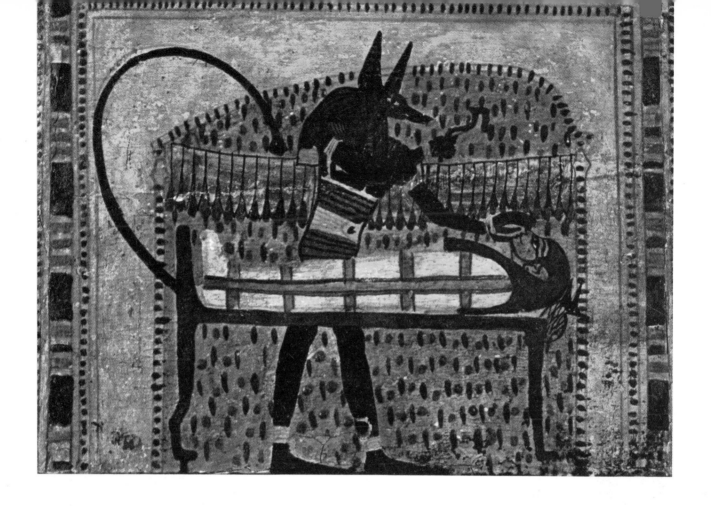

THE SPIRIT THAT LIVES ON

The twilight of Egyptian civilisation had come. The sun, a golden disk with the head of Râ, sank beneath the Nile, shedding its last rays over the jagged shadow of the proud palm-trees. The stillness of evening spread over Egypt.

At this moment, the whole of life became silent. The river lapped weakly against its banks, the feluccas, their sails now lowered, lay huddled together at the water's edge. Far away, the warm desert wind began to rise, rustling among the dunes.

Then the dead came out of their tombs. The ghostly shadows of the gods took possession of the temples, and the crowds of yester-year flocked into the courtyard. The flutes sounded, and, to loud acclaim, the Pharaoh's procession advanced between two rows of enigmatic sphinxes.

Every night, the gods of the old Egypt are reborn, like Isis and Osiris, and the desert echoes their plaintive tones. Time had buried them. asleep, under the sands. And 20th century man has buried them under water. How many monuments now lie, hidden for ever, under the blue-green waters of Lake Nasser? The inexorable march of technical progress does not allow time for the quest for hidden beauty and the lost words of antiquity.

Yet the spirit of the old Egypt remains. Past century upon century, despite invasions, barbarians and the vicissitudes of history, the wisdom of the priests of Memphis and Thebes has come down to us. Through Pythagoras, the Greek philosophers and the Roman Empire. their heritage has been forwarded to us.

Paul Valéry wrote: "We civilisations know that we are mortal... Across the vast reaches of time, we have seen the phantoms of immense vessels which had once been laden with wealth and brilliance..."

No! Egyptian civilization is not dead; it lives on within each Western man and woman, whether or not they realize it. Because the lush banks of the ancient Nile were the starting point from which a breath of wisdom, balance and greatness, having swept across the Mediterranean, has enabled Europe for more than two thousand years, to be the radiant, glorious beacon of human progress.

May Râ be blessed!